# I ATTACKED PEARL HARBOR

**Ensign Kazuo Sakamaki**

Translated by Toru Matsumoto
Annotated by Gary R. Coover

**Rollston Press**

*I Attacked Pearl Harbor*

by Ensign Kazuo Sakamaki

ISBN-13: 978-0-9970748-4-0

ISBN-10: 0-9970748-4-1

Cover photo courtesy of US Navy

**Rollston Press**
1717 Ala Wai Blvd, Suite 1703
Honolulu, HI 96815

*"We had no hatred of the Americans"*


*"The enemy was our opponent in battle"*


*"The most important thing for us was to die manfully on the battlefield – as the petals of the cherry blossoms fall to the ground – and that in war there is only victory and no retreat"*


*"I wish to preach to no one. I only hope that this will show to all others who were once prisoners and to all who have received us with varying moods that man is capable of being made anew."*

# *Contents*

PREFACE TO THE NEW EDITION

Foreword        9

Introduction        11

1.  On to Pearl Harbor!        15

2.  Struggle for Death        36

3.  Struggle for Life        46

4.  On the Surface, Harmony        72

5.  Talk on Suicide        84

6.  From War to Peace in Japan        103

7.  Love and the Beginning of Freedom        113

8.  Skinny but Happy        119


APPENDIX

      The Submarine Attack on Pearl Harbor
      The Five Midget Subs
      The Nine Hero Gods
      Sakamaki's Post WWII Career
      Recommended Reading
      Acknowledgements
      Toru Matsumoto, Translator
      Gary R. Coover, Editor

# PREFACE TO THE NEW EDITION

The midget submarine attack on Pearl Harbor is a little-known part of the Imperial Japanese Navy's surprise attack on the United States Pacific Fleet on December 7, 1941.

Five specially-designed, fast, battery-powered top secret 2-man submarines were deployed for the first time in modern warfare to augment the aerial torpedoing and bombardment by attacking the enemy from below.

Launched outside the harbor from larger mother submarines, these midgets met with limited success. One, and maybe two, actually managed to get inside Pearl Harbor in the attack on Battleship Row.

This is the story of one of the midget submarine officers for whom fortune was not smiling that day – mechanical troubles and alert defenders managed to prevent his 2-man submarine from entering the harbor. Its troubles continued for the next 24-hours, resulting in finally running aground on a reef on the far side of Oahu, the death of one of its crew, and the capture of its skipper and the top-secret submarine itself by American military personnel.

Ensign Kazuo Sakamaki subsequently became American Prisoner of War #1 and spent the next several years in various POW camps across the United States.

He returned to Japan after the end of the war to much publicity and scorn, but returned a much-changed man from the blindly militaristic young sailor who had left Japan four years earlier on a sacred mission for his Emperor and his country.

At age 29 he wrote an account of his time in the navy and in the camps, and that is what you have before you today, translated from the original Japanese into English and originally published as *I Attacked Pearl Harbor* by the International Committee of Young Men's Christian Associations in 1949.

Along with the addition of a few contemporary photographs, annotations and some supplementary historical information, every word of the original book is included and formatted exactly as printed in 1949. The language and syntax are a bit archaic at times, and the story rambles a bit here and there, but the important thing to remember is these are the thoughts and words of a young Japanese sailor with a very unique viewpoint of a critical time in American and world history.

Long out of print, you are now able to enjoy this memoir once again and come away with a better understanding of the motivations, the regrets and the hopes experienced by young Ensign Kazuo Sakamaki.

GARY R. COOVER
Rollston Press, 2017
Honolulu

# *Foreword*

As Mr. Nara explains in his introduction, the whole story is as Japanese as can be. In translating it I have done nothing to alter the connotation of any word originally used by the author. "The China Incident" appears as "the China Incident." The submarine skipper's desire to risk his life "for the peace of the world" is there as he had expressed it – just as he must have felt it in his heart.

Some aspects of a prisoner's life, such as the thoughts of and on suicide, seem overweighted. The author's treatment of his love for a refugee girl from Hiroshima seems too indirect and cumbersome. But that is what makes this story so genuine. I would not change one line of it.

A translator is not responsible for contents. But may I add that I have seldom read (or translated) so true a story as this. It is not the best or the easiest book I have tried to translate, but while working on it I have very closely lived with the author mentally, nodding and shaking my head alternately, but always admiring his honesty.

Tsutae Nara is a general secretary of the Y.M.C.A. of Osaka, Japan. His close friendship with the author and his familiarity with the problems of other demobilized soldiers of Japan, whom he is helping to rehabilitate and adjust to civilian life under the Occupation, make him particularly qualified to introduce this book.

TORU MATSUMOTO

Larchmont, New York
1949

# *Introduction*

By the providence of God, the United States of America and Japan are today inseparable partners in a unique experiment in the history of human social evolution. America, representing the Allies in World War II, is playing the role of teacher and stimulus. Japan, totally defeated and repentant, is a willing and co-operative pupil. What eventually will emerge out of this experience may determine the shape of things to come in the Pacific for many centuries.

The peoples of other countries have been kept informed of the development in Japan by official reports, books, and magazine articles written by non-Japanese authors. They have portrayed the picture from the standpoint of democratic principles and practices well understood in the West. While this serves a useful purpose, it does not and cannot reveal the inner revolution in the mind of the Japanese. Yet an understanding of this inner change is essential for a full appreciation of the current drama in Japan.

A relatively easy thing to do would be to let some-one who is a Japanese speak for the people of Japan –

someone who knows the western mind and interprets the Japanese mind in terms of western concepts. But a shortcoming of such an attempt is immediately self-evident. He would write with the Occidental reader in mind. He would omit things that he felt were irrelevant to the West. Because he is likely to be familiar with democratic concepts, he will interpret Japanese concepts in the same terms and present his material as either good or bad in the western frame of reference. The consequence would be a partial presentation of the Japanese mind.

Soon after the end of the war a small book was published in Japan. This book, *Four Years as Prisoner-of-War Number One*, was different from all other post-war volumes in Japan in one very important respect: the author did not claim that he had always believed in democracy. In fact it was a frank statement of personal feelings and experiences of a young submarine officer in the Japanese navy. What attracted the public attention was the fact that he was the first Japanese to be captured as a prisoner of the United States. The book was an instant sensation and best-seller.

When I read the book I was struck by one thing – the author's utter sincerity. Later, as I reflected upon the psychological development of the young naval officer, a significant truth dawned upon me: it is possible for a Japanese youth educated for ruthless war to become a normal person. Here, a man who had received the most rigorous military education and who spearheaded the attack on Pearl Harbor, changed, while a prisoner of war, from a beastlike, inhuman creature to a real human being. After he returned to Japan, where he was ridiculed and intimidated because he had not met an honorable soldier's death in fighting or suicide, he found the meaning of freedom and the way to a happy, constructive life through marriage and a useful occupation, both of his own choice. There cannot be a truer presentation of the problem and hope of the younger generation of Japan than the story in this book.

Since coming to America at the invitation of the International Committee of the Y.M.C.A.'s and of the International Association of Y's Men's Clubs, I have told the story of Mr. Kazuo Sakamaki, author of the book entitled in Japan, *Four Years as Prisoner-of-War Number One*. I have told it to thousands of people at Y.M.C.A.'s, churches, clubs, and schools. I have been impressed by the interest shown in the experiences of Kazuo Sakamaki. Many of my American friends have urged me to make the book available in English.

Since it was my good fortune to know the author personally, I was able to persuade him to consent to a translation of his book. He was most hesitant at first, saying the book was not meant for western readers. I stressed the value of the very fact that it had not been written for them. He finally agreed.

Because the original material was somewhat dated and incomplete, I asked him to enlarge on two important parts of his life: how he obtained his naval training and how he feels about Japan today. He replied in the form of a letter to me, written as if he were talking to a Japanese friend of his, which is now incorporated into the book.

I believe that Mr. Sakamaki's story is a valuable one because he has no ax to grind. He writes as a Japanese talking always to Japanese. He hides nothing. He does not speak as a Christian because he is not one. He does not speak as a convinced believer in democracy because he is not one. He is truly honest with himself.

Having obtained the material and edited it into shape, there was the question of translation. Judging from the contents of the material, written in simple Japanese but rather indirectly expressed, I did not feel justified in calling on a translator whose mother tongue was not Japanese. Yet the transmission of the inner thoughts of an alien mind to readers in the West seemed to require experience in the handling of the intricate problem of translating without transcending the author's intent. I have solved this problem by turning over the story to Toru Matsumoto who thinks and writes in the two languages as naturally as if he had been born in both countries. I trust that my choice and judgment prove to have been correct!

I shall be back in Japan by the time this volume reaches the public in the West. My full-time work is with the youth of Japan through the Y.M.C.A. I shall welcome letters from friends in the United States and Canada and all other countries who wish to know more about the youth of Japan, or about Mr. Sakamaki.

THOMAS TSUTAE NARA

Chicago, 1949

# 1. *On to Pearl Harbor!*

On the morning of November 16, 1941, we of the Special Attack Forces were ordered to assemble in the private room of the naval command of the Kure Base[1].

As we stood at attention, Vice-admiral Shimizu spoke solemnly.

"These are the orders from the headquarters of the General Staff of the Imperial Navy. You are herewith directed to take positions of readiness for war with the United States of America."

It was cold in that room. When those words registered themselves in my mind, I was astonished and felt as if suddenly petrified. The effect was like a sudden magic blow.

A sheet of paper was handed to each one of us. It was a written order which had been just given orally. With this paper in our hands, there was no longer any doubt.

"War with America!"

---

[1] The Kure Naval District located on the Inland Sea in Hiroshima Prefecture was Japan's largest naval base from 1889 to 1945. [Ed.]

The thought was gripping.

Vice-admiral Shimizu, commander of the Sixth Fleet to which our third squadron belonged, proceeded to give separate and supplementary orders to the commander of the Special (Suicide) Attack Forces under him and to the skipper of each ship. Everyone maintained strict, stoic silence. Once in a while someone cleared his throat or let out a heavy sigh. Someone laughed, but it was a weak laugh that died in the raw and grim atmosphere of the room.

The admiral faced us again.

"Now listen very carefully. The X-Day, the day to open hostilities, is set for December 8[2]; the time, daybreak. The order to open fire will be issued by the General Staff of the navy in Tokyo, just before the time set for attack. Under no circumstances are you to take action unless ordered."

We looked at the sheets in our hands again. The positions our ships were to take were clearly shown.

Then Admiral Shimizu concluded:

"One mistake on the part of anyone of you may be fatal to all of us – the Sixth Fleet, the navy itself, and the whole country. I trust in your loyalty and ability. Best of luck to you. And now, will you meet me at the club for lunch?"

We left the room. I walked downstairs in a daze, as if a heavy hammer had struck me in the head.

"It has finally come," I thought. My whole body was filled with strange pain.

The more I thought about it, the more fixed the

---

[2] Japanese time is one day ahead of United States time. [Ed.]

16

reality of the situation seemed. I composed myself and made ready to depart.

We had lunch with Admiral Shimizu at the naval officer's club called the Suikosha. Toasts for success were exchanged.

The next day I took a walk with Ensign Hirowo, a classmate of mine from the Naval Academy, through the city of Kure.

"This is our last night in Japan, Ensign," I said.

"You are right. When we go, we cannot expect to return," replied my companion thoughtfully.

We were members of a suicide squadron. We did not know how we could ever come back alive.

We saw a small bottle of perfume in a store window.

"Ensign, here is something we must have." I pointed to the bottle.

"Perfume! Yes, we must have it," he agreed.

So we each bought one bottle. Japanese warriors in the old days went to battle attired in their best armor and perfumed, in order to be fit for a sudden and glorious death, like "cherry blossoms falling to the ground."

We held hands firmly and prayed for each other's success.

On the eighteenth I wrote a letter to my parents – it was my birthday.

"I am now leaving," I wrote. "I owe you, my parents, a debt I shall never be able to repay. Whatever may happen to me, it is in the service of our country that I go. Words cannot express my gratitude for the privilege of fighting for the cause of peace and justice."

If my words seemed impersonal, it was because at the moment of departing from the land of my birth, I was saying good-by to all things to which a normal person clings. I had made up my mind to cease being normal. I, Kazuo Sakamaki, was being buried as of that moment. A skipper of a secret submarine going out in the service of his country was dictating that letter. I swallowed tears in my mouth.

At noon our submarine, which carried my midget submarine on her, slipped out of Kure.

By the evening of that day we arrived at Nasaka Jima, a small island in the Inland Sea where we completed preparation in every detail and left the island, with our compass set for Pearl Harbor.

On the nineteenth I stood on the deck and watched the coastal hills disappear in the deepening darkness. When I realized that this was my last glimpse of Japan, I could not help tears flowing out of my eyes.

"Good-by, Japan," I whispered, "Good-by"

I was not crying in mere sorrow. Everyone aboard the submarine seemed highly excited. As I looked about, I saw color in their cheeks. They all stood proudly as the salty wind of the sea fluttered their uniforms.

My only companion in the midget submarine was a younger petty officer and he was officially my aide. Each day he and I went into our craft and worked on our plan.

When we approached Wake Island, we submerged during the day though continuing our movement without letup. At night we sailed on the surface.

Once I was washed overboard by the powerful waves of the Pacific. Fortunately I had tied myself by a rope so that I was able to get back to the ship.

The squadron cut through between Wake and Midway and charted its course directly toward Hawaii.

On December 5 [hereafter all dates are American] I saw the islands of Hawaii. We paused and turned the radio on. Unfamiliar jazz music came in.

"This must be from Honolulu," I said.

"Yes, sir," my comrade returned grimly.

"This means we are in the enemy water now."

"Yes, sir."

The radio music gave me a queer feeling.

Everything seemed to be working smoothly. But that night I discovered a horrifying fact: my all-important gyrocompass was out of order. Now it was impossible for the midget submarine to move under sea. This was a matter of utmost seriousness. Without the smooth operation of this compass, failure and death were certain. I was at my wit's end.

On the night of December 5 we received radio instructions giving the locations of all the ships of the Pacific Fleet within Pearl Harbor on that very day[3]. See Figure 1 for the information given to us. The actual line-up was as in Figure 2. There were such differences! How this discrepancy occurred I did not know. It did not, of course, occur to me that the information from Tokyo (that is where it had come

---

[3] Although the naval striking force maintained strict radio silence between Japan and Hawaii, they could still listen to and receive coded messages from Tokyo. [Ed.]

from) could be so wrong.

When night came on the sixth, I saw through the telescope the red and green lights of Pearl Harbor. We were approximately twenty miles south of the entrance to the great naval base of the United States Pacific Fleet and were moving straight into the target – Pearl Harbor! The sky above us was filled with stars. The waves of the ocean were restless about us.

In a few hours our midget submarine would be released from the mother ship. My heart beat faster. I packed my personal effects, wrote a letter of farewell to father, cleaned my body, changed into the uniform of the midget submarine, and sprayed the perfume on it. This was the preparation of death. With my compass out of order it was more than a matter of ceremonial formality. I expected to die.

The captain showed me a message which he had just received form Admiral Isoroku Yamamoto, commander in chief of the entire attacking fleet. It said:

"The moment has arrived. The rise or fall of our empire is at stake. Everyone do his duty."

Through the loud-speaker system the captain spoke:

"We are about to carry out the Hawaii operation as scheduled. All hands be ready."

Captain Hanabusa turned to me and asked:

"Ensign Sakamaki, we have arrived at our destination, but your gyrocompass is not working. What are you going to do?"

To this I replied without hesitation:

"Captain, I am going ahead!"

"On to Pearl Harbor!" the captain shouted.

"On to Pearl Harbor!" I echoed.

I entered my midget submarine.

I looked through the telescope and mentally charted the course I wanted to take. I trusted in my luck. Such action was reckless, and yet I could not see how I could miss. I was optimism itself. The target was right in front of me, and I was going to attack it. This was not entirely empty courage.

"After all," I said to myself, "I have come all the way from Japan within the sight of success. How can I quit and return?"

I thought of my parents. They would be ashamed if I should fail. I thought of my brother who was in the army. What would he think of me? Then all these years of preparation and training...

"I cannot fail. I simply cannot fail."

Ever since I was a small boy, I dreamed of doing something heroic for my country, and the moment of glory was at hand. Ever since I was a small boy...

*  *  *

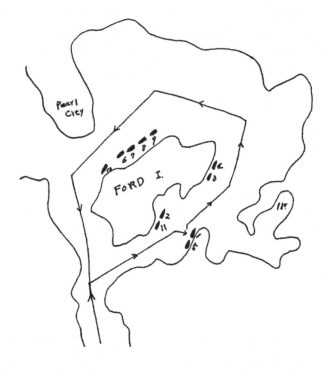

Fig. 1

Made by Kazuo Sakamaki

The plan for submarine attack on Pearl Harbor

These positions of the warships were given by the Naval General Staff in Tokyo on December 5, 1941 to the squadron.

1. Pennsylvania
2. Maryland
3. Tennessee
4. California
5. Arizona
6. Wyoming

7. San Francisco
8. Omaha
9. Trenton
10. Saratoga
11. West Virginia

22

Fig. 2

The actual positions of United States warships in Pearl Harbor at the time of the attack.

| | |
|---|---|
| 1. Pennsylvania | 14. Utah |
| 2. West Virginia | 15. St. Louis |
| 3. Tennessee | 16. Honolulu |
| 4. California | 17. Helena |
| 5. Arizona | 18. Oglala |
| 11. Oklahoma | 19. Curtis |
| 12. Maryland | 20. Solage |
| 13. Nevada | 21. Shaw |

November 18, 1918, one week after the end of World War I, was when I was born. My parents lived in a small village on Shikoku Island.

"We will call him Kazuo," father said, I was told. Kazuo meant "peace boy, and it was fitting that the son be named in commemorization of the coming of peace.

The village was a quiet place, surrounded by beautiful hills and gentle rivers. I spent nearly twenty years in this peaceful environment until I finish high school. Peaceful, yes, as far as the physical surroundings were concerned.

Like all other children of Japan, I faithfully obeyed my parents and teachers, who wished me to grow up to be a fine man. My boyhood was filled with happiness.

I remembered how I heard Japanese mythological tales. Even when I discovered that the Japanese stories were mere legends, I wanted to believe them just as they had been taught, because I thought it was the right thing to do. Besides there seemed to be no need to disbelieve. Japan was a wonderful country to have had such a beautiful beginning.

When I was still in school the Manchurian Incident of 1931[4] occurred, followed later by the China Incident of 1937[5]. I remembered how our village was filled with martial air as we went to see soldiers off.

"Banzai! Banzai!" we shouted.

We sang the national anthem and waved the flags of

---

[4] The Manchurian Incident was an event staged by the Japanese military as an excuse to invade northeastern China. [Ed.]

[5] Also known as the Marco Polo Bridge Incident which began as a dispute between Japanese and Chinese troops near Beijing which started the Second Sino-Japanese War. [Ed.]

the Rising Sun to encourage our soldiers.

As the conditions in the nation changed, my ideas were gradually, but inevitably, modified by them. The thing I heard most was the phrase "national emergency."

People said, "Every fine young man will become a good soldier and serve the country." I heard this both at home and at school, and friends said it and books repeated it. The change was not sudden, and because it was not, our whole thinking moved along with it. As my father was a schoolteacher, I had always wanted to follow in his footsteps, but now, like most children around me, I, too, wanted to become a soldier.

"The soldier" was, however, an idea, a concept. My ideal was the man in the smartest uniform of the Naval Academy. That was the dream of every young man in Japan.

One day, while I was still in high school, I came home and said to my parents:

"Father and mother, everyone at school is going to join the army or navy. I wish to enter the Naval Academy. May I?"

"The Naval Academy!" my parents said, astonished.

"Yes, that's where the country's best boys go."

"But son, it's a difficult place to enter."

My family were apprehensive. Not that they were opposed to the career of a naval officer, but they were not sure that I had what it would take. All my ancestors had been civilians – village officials and schoolteachers – and my parents wondered if there was enough military mettle in me.

Relatives were called in and they pondered the question. They asked my teacher if I could make it. Finally they agreed to let me try.

Six thousand boys from all over Japan applied for admission to the Naval Academy. Ninety-five per cent of them were rejected after competitive examinations based on intellectual and physical qualifications. I could not believe it when I discovered that I was among the fortunate three hundred who passed the narrow gate.

On April 1, 1937, I became a full-fledged student of the Naval Academy. It was just before the outbreak of the Marco Polo Incident, that later developed into the China Incident.

The school was located on Eta Jima, a small island in the Inland Sea, the most beautiful part of Japan, with evergreen pines and blue water all seasons of the year. This was Japan's Annapolis for the training of future naval officers. Life was rigorous.

Often, when we were rowing our cutter, our hands bled and our underpants were smeared with blood. But we rowed on. We charged our boat into a fierce storm, and if we vomited in anguish we did not turn back. When we were on land we practiced wrestling, rising up from the floor even when we could hardly breathe through exhaustion. These were, however, mere physical hardships – all in the course of training.

Our mental exercises were also exacting. Not only were we required to learn the subjects offered in a regular college, but we were also required to master all branches of knowledge connected with military life. In classroom work alone we had thirty-six hours a week. Six members of my class became sick and had to drop out.

Perhaps our spiritual discipline was not as rigid as it was at the Military Academy. But we were taught, and we came to believe, that the most important things for us was to die manfully on the battlefield – as the petals of the cherry blossoms fall to the ground – and that in war there is only victory and no retreat. There was, however, technique in both, and that was why we were in the special school.

As we continued in this rigorous routing, the China Incident spread wider and wider, and the international atmosphere became darker by the month. With this development in the larger world moving ahead all around us, it became increasingly clear to some of us that there was no room for individual thinking and that absolute obedience to our superiors was the only behavior becoming a cadet. There was no more time to think about, let alone look at, flowers in the field, or to consider the question of life or death. The weight of duty and the sense of responsibility filled my mind. This meant that I had to rule out all thoughts of pleasures of life and concentrate on becoming an instrument for world peace even if that should require fiercely fighting in war.

I was told that if there should be a global war, our opponents would be the navies of the United States and Great Britain. To us, therefore, the great adversary would be the United States fleet, the strongest in the world. Our officer-instructors told us what Annapolis of America and Dartmouth of England were like, how the cadets were trained there: "Just as rigorously, if not more so, than you are." All this stirred up in me a fighting spirit.

Our naval authorities knew that the Japanese navy was not equal to the combined forces of the United States and Great Britain. They told us so. In order to fight a superior force, a special combat technique was necessary. This was sudden attack. This would require the supreme sacrifice on the part of every Japanese taking part – a suicidal death.

I was graduated in August, 1940, and was commissioned a midshipman. Instead of the world-wide cruise which was customary up to that time, we spent two months in a maneuver near the China coast, in the Japan Sea, and in the western Pacific. We received, for one month, training in air-flight.

My career in my smartest uniform began when I was assigned to a light cruiser, the *Abukuma*, the flagship of the torpedo squadron. I was a gun officer for a month, and later, when we sailed to Formosa and Saigon, I was a deck officer.

On April 1, 1941, I received orders from the Minister of the Navy. I was promoted to ensign and ordered to report to the *Chiyoda*, the mystery ship of December 7, 1941.

When I reported to the captain of the ship, Kaku Harada[6], the commanding officer told us, "Fellows, you are going to receive a very special type of training from now on." The captain asked our pledge to keep it an absolute secret because "you are going in a secret weapon – the midget submarine."

I was given a week's vacation and I went home. I tried not to show any anxiety to my family. But when I said good-by, there was a feeling that this might be the last time I would see my father and mother.

That the personnel of the midget submarine group was selected with the utmost care was obvious. The twenty-four, picked from the entire Japanese navy, had in common: bodily strength and physical energy; determination and fighting spirit; freedom from family care. They were unmarried and from large families.

None of us was a volunteer. We had all been ordered to our assignment. That none of us objected goes without saying: we know that punishment would be very severe if we objected; we were supposed to feel highly honored.

The *Chiyoda* belonged to the First Fleet group, and was anchored near the naval shipyard at Kure. She had been a seaplane tender and was undergoing conversion

---

[6] Harada, then captain, remained a training officer throughout the war and died in a detention camp in the Philippines.

for the purpose of carrying and launching midget submarines. We slept on board during the night and went to the Kure naval torpedo laboratory during the day to study the midget submarine then under construction.

I was told that a naval engineer had conceived the idea of a midget ship in 1927 and that the first model had been constructed in 1929. It remained in the laboratory during the period when Japan was reducing her armaments and peace sentiment was strong in the country. Experimental work was continued under Commander Kato (who later died in the Philippines), who studied the problem of making the invention practicable. In 1935 the midget submarine received its first showing in the headquarters of the navy's high command. It was in 1940 that the first stage of practical use was reached. In the fall of the same year Captain Naoji Iwasa and Commander Saburo Akieda and other commanded the first midget submarine in an undersea training test. By March, 1941, the training of the first group was complete with convincing results. Now, I and the others in this group were ready to receive training from them.

For the interior of the forty-six ton midget submarine, see Figure 3 on page 32.

The special feature, besides its size, was the speed of twenty-four knots in a forward movement either under or above water. This underwater craft was supposed to be the fastest of its kind in the world. From its nickname, "a two-man sub," it is clear that it was manned by two men only.

We were told that this submarine would be used in three special ways:

1.  To attack an enemy's largest ship at the very first moment of an encounter with an enemy fleet. This was to be a sudden and surprise attack.
2.  To attack, similarly, a large enemy ship by secretly entering a harbor or naval base of an enemy.
3.  To be used as a "trump card" as occasion might arise.

We considered the first of the three as being the most important, and studied its many ramifications.

We imagined that a war with the United States would go something like this: As soon as hostilities broke out, the Japanese troops and the marines of the navy would want to land on and occupy the Philippine Islands. The United States would then want to send reinforcements there. This would mean a large convoy accompanied by the main Pacific Fleet of the U.S. Navy going south-westward across the Pacific. The Japanese fleet would intercept this in mid-ocean in an all-out effort to prevent it from reaching the objective and at the same time to reduce the fighting ability of the U.S. fleet at least to the level of parity with the Japanese fleet.

In such an encounter, without necessarily physical contact of the two opposing forces in terms of warships, there would first be a fight for the control of the air, accompanied by torpedo attacks. During this stage of the fighting, our midget submarines would be secretly released from thirty miles distance for the purpose of blowing up the main battleships of the enemy formation.

While we thought up all sorts of strategy in war, we spent most of our time in improving our technical skills. We did this at the submarine school in Kure naval base, paying special attention to the problem of a surprise attack against a large craft.

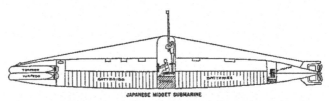

Fig. 3. Japanese Midget Submarine.

Length overall .. 78 ft., 10 in.
Diameter ....... 6 ft., 6 in.
Displacement ........46 tons
Speed (submerged) 24 knots
Engine ...... electric motor
Radius:
    24 knots = 90 minutes
    4 knots = 100 miles

Speed gears:
    1st .......... 24 knots
    2nd .......... 10 knots
    3rd .......... 6 knots
    4th .......... 4 knots
Go stern .......... 4 knots
Arms ..... 2 18 in.-torpedoes

I became a trained submarine skipper. In June, 1941, I manned my own ship and started realistic maneuvers from a base at a small fishing village called Mitsukuye in the Inland Sea. I spent all my time learning how to operate and use it in a sudden attack. I relied upon the extreme difficulty of my ship's being discovered because of its smallness and high speed. I tried to perfect my skill in attacking, so that my performance would be 100 per cent accurate. With two torpedoes at my disposal I was confident that I could get my target without failure.

While this training was going on, we were closely

guarded and well treated. There were many times when we were in danger of accident, but we were always watched by regular torpedo boats or some other patrolling surface crafts which followed us. We sometimes collided with one another. We were grounded more than once. But the personnel suffered no casualties. By the end of September, 1941, we had completed our training and were ready for any emergency.

During October I gathered from the words and behavior of our superiors that something serious was in the air. Our maneuvers shifted from a mid-ocean encounter to an inside-harbor tactic. Captain Harada showed us maps of Hong Kong, Singapore, Sidney, San Francisco, and Pearl Harbor.

"Learn the peculiarities of these harbors," said the captain.

"Commit them to your memory."

During the middle of October we were stationed on the north coast of Shikoku facing the Inland Sea. There we practiced techniques of invading a narrow inlet at night. While we were receiving this specialized training, we could not help speculating that perhaps in the event of war we might take part in an inside-bay attack by slipping into an enemy harbor at night.

At the beginning of November we were given another week of vacation. Previously we were merely going home for a furlough. This time, a week at home had been prefaced by this advice:

"We may go on a long maneuver. Say good-by to your parents."

An indescribable fear of real war crept into my mind as I went home to meet my family. "This time it may be the real thing," I said to myself.

Saying good-by was not easy, even for a submarine skipper who had had training in suppressing emotions. I could hardly look at my parents. Though my family and friends said they were proud of me, I was unable to look them straight in the face and smile with them. That they were proud of me I did not doubt. But the thought of never seeing them again was overpowering. When I had to part from them, the moment which had been reserved for glory was an hour of agony.

When I returned from home, we five officers and five petty officers were ordered to go on board the five first-class submarines which composed the Third Submarine Squadron, anchored in Kure. My ship was Submarine A-24[7]. As soon as I reported to A-24, Commander Yoshita Hanabusa issued orders to me to get ready to sail. I and the four other skippers loaded our midget submarines with food and ammunition on board the mother submarine. All this was done very speedily and, of course, in utter secrecy.

Then that fateful morning of November 16 – the serious look on the admiral's face, the grim atmosphere of the room.

"Readiness for war with the United States!"

The farewell lunch with Admiral Shimizu. A walk through Kure. Perfume.

\* \* \*

---

[7] Perhaps an error in translation, this submarine was known as "I-24", commissioned on October 31, 1941. [Ed.]

34

We reached our objective without being detected. Everything and everyone had exact positions and functions. There was no room for a margin of error. Even though the important gyrocompass of my submarine was out of order, my position in this grand scheme of assault did not allow me any thought of running away from death, which was now more certain than ever. I was securely bound by duty to perform according to orders, and to that end I had to marshal my spirits regardless of probable consequences. I shook off all nonsense from myself like a good warrior. I had never seen death. I had never witnessed any tragedy of war. I was like a young warrior facing battle for the first time. If I thought about death, it did not frighten me at all. In fact I smiled like a hero about to subdue a superior adversary.

About ten miles southwest of the mouth of Pearl Harbor, my midget submarine was released from the mother submarine under submerged conditions. It was eleven o'clock on the night of December 6.

The moment had come.

My family, my village, the navy, and my country – they were depending on me.

From this moment I was on my own. The target was right ahead. I had to make good. If I should succeed, well and good. If I should fail? No! I could not fail. With death I would accomplish my objective.

On to Pearl Harbor!

# 2. *Struggle for Death*

SOMETHING went wrong.

At the moment of release, my submarine nearly toppled over into the water. The trim had not worked well. I feared that if we attempted to emerge hastily, enemy observers might spot the ship. I remembered that the opening of hostilities was to follow the handing of the notice of war to the United States government. If by my own mistake the presence of the Japanese forces should be discovered, it would create a grave problem. It would spoil the surprise air attack and every other detail of the carefully worked-out plan. I could not cause such a blunder. No matter how dangerous the condition of my ship, I could not let it emerge to the surface.

My aide and I crawled back and forth inside the submarine, removing the lead ballast and filling the tanks with water to correct the trim of the craft. It had been our plan that by midnight all five submarines would be inside the harbor and would sink to the bottom and wait for the dawn. But when I looked at the watch, it was midnight already. The ship righted itself.

I figured that as long as we entered the harbor during the night, no damage would have been done. I drank a bit of wine and ate my lunch.

"Let's do our utmost!" My aide and I held each other's hands and pledged success. I took my position and moved forward with minimum speed.

After ten minutes I lifted the ship up slightly to see through the telescope where we were going. What did I see? To my horror, the ship was moving in the wrong direction!

Moving blindly because my gyrocompass was not working, the ship had gone ninety degrees off her course. If I could manage the ship with the help of the telescope, we could get back on our course, but this was clearly impossible.

"We must get to the mouth of the harbor," I repeated to myself. My hands were wet with cold sweat. I changed the direction three or four times, hoping against hope that somehow the ship would get going where I wanted to go. The speed was maintained at the minimum as before.

Heaven was not on my side. No matter how hard I tried, we could not approach the entrance of the harbor. We were moving about in total blindness, the night was spent, and the fatal morning was coming upon us. When I looked, the island of Oahu was clearly visible. I saw two U.S. patrol craft going back and forth. They were guarding the entrance to the harbor.

Time ticked away in complete indifference to my predicament. It was almost the moment for attack.

I thought about the other four midget subs. They were supposed to be going on their own to their respective targets. But I did not know where they were nor could I see them. Besides I was too preoccupied with my own problem.

My aide turned an anxious face towards me. I wanted to show him my determination and give him encouragement. So I said:

"Have no fear. Now that we have come this far, it is our duty to do our task. We will somehow break through that guard line and pierce into the enemy harbor. Once inside it, we will dare to run the surface. Then we will let our torpedoes go at an enemy battle-ship. If necessary, let's dash into one of them. That's our mission. In a few hours our fate will be decided. So cheer up."

My aide gave a big nod.

I became bolder after my little speech. I raised the ship to a depth of about thirty-five feet and in complete blindness moved toward the patrol guard line. The sun was out and the waves reflected the light sharply.

As we came nearer to the enemy ships guarding the entrance, I was able to see the white uniforms of the sailors aboard. The enemy ships had four funnels each. I first thought that they might be light cruisers, but from the shapes of the funnels and the construction of the bridge and the stern decks, I concluded they were destroyers.

"Just a couple of destroyers," I told myself in artificial contempt. I pushed the midget submarine toward them. Then suddenly I heard an enormous noise and felt the ship shaking. I was hit on my head and lost consciousness. This was my first contact with war.

I came to myself in a short while and saw white smoke in my submarine. I change the speed to half gear and turned the ship around. I wanted to see if any damage had been done to the ship. My aide was all right. The two torpedoes were all right. So I got ready to try again to break through the destroyers. I did not want to waste my torpedoes on those destroyers which began again to charge against me. They threw depth charges at us. They fell near us but not as close as the first time. I had to speed up again and turn the ship for the second time.

I decided that it was the height of stupidity to continue this blind action. The only sensible thing to do was to get out on the surface and go straight ahead toward the target and death. I looked through the telescope and hated the sight of the two destroyers. I turned my eyes toward the harbor and saw several columns of black smoke! I was hot throughout my body. I breathed faster, and my heart was beating at a terrific speed. I held on to my telescope and shouted to my aide:

"They've done it! Look at it!"

The scene of the attack greatly aroused my companion. He shouted with joy:

"The air raid! A great success! Look at that smoke! Enemy ships are burning. We must do our best, too, and we will!"

We set our course again and began our move. I gave orders to the aide, "Next time we are hit, we are not going to turn around. We are going straight ahead."

The destroyers with white foam rising behind came charging toward us.

Depth charges fell upon us and the ship nearly turned over.

"You idiots!" I condemned the destroyers and kept the course straight and steady towards the mouth of the harbor.

Bang!

I knew what had happened. The ship had got stuck on the coral reef. Now the whole submarine was exposed to the enemy. What a blunder I had committed just one step short of the goal! I looked back and saw the destroyers still going back and forth. I had to extricate the submarine in a hurry from this awkward position. I used the maximum backward power and, after four attempts, succeeded in getting back into the water.

I looked at the torpedoes. One of them was so badly damaged that it was of no use any more.

The compressed air and gas from the battery were leaking, and the air inside the submarine was reaching forty pounds and becoming dangerously foul. We were very tired and weary.

It was near noon. We had not done anything. I was getting very restless. The two destroyers looked as if they were two big cats playing with a little mouse. I wanted to sink one of them with the last of my torpedoes, which would have been as easy as killing a bird in the palm, but my target was not such a tiny ship. I still wanted to get a battleship. The *Pennsylvania*, flagship of the U.S. Pacific Fleet, was my object.[8]

I made a second attempt to get to the entrance. As expected, we were hit again. We pushed forward, nevertheless, and for a moment I thought we had succeeded in getting through. But heaven was on the other side. The ship hit a coral reef at the port entrance for the second time.

As in the previous time I applied the maximum backward power, but this time nothing happened.

"This might be our end," we said to each other.

We moved the lead ballast from the front to the rear. Because the battery was overflowing, we received electric shocks as we crawled back and forth on the flooded floor. How long our desperate efforts to get off the coral reef lasted, I do not remember. It seemed like several hours. A destroyer started firing at us, we were told later, but we did not hear any loud explosions at all at the time.

Miraculously we got our ship afloat again. We lowered the ship deep and started investigating the damages. Then we discovered a fatal injury to the torpedo-discharging mechanism. No longer was the sole weapon at our disposal useful to us. Our only hope was gone. An attack without a torpedo was meaningless.

"What are we going to do, sir?" My aide asked, anxiously.

"The only thing we can do now is to plunge right into the *Pennsylvania*," I answered, almost crossly.

---

[8] Unbeknownst to Sakamaki, the USS *Pennsylvania* was in dry dock in Pearl Harbor at the time of the attack. [Ed.]

My aide knew that it meant our self-destruction as well.

"If we can't blast the enemy battleship, we will climb onto it and kill as many enemies as possible."

"Yes, sir."

I made up my mind to do just that. But the realization that I had failed tortured my mind and bitter tears rolled down my face incessantly. It was past noon, and if we should delay any more, the dark curtain of night would fall. With perspiration drenching my body, I started the ship towards the mouth of the harbor for the last time. I must have been half out of my mind. I did not care. I could not think. I just tried and tried. I was working blindly. I do not remember the rest of the afternoon.

The night came. It was dark everywhere. Everything had failed. My aide was crying. I was still holding the telescope. I could not utter a word. I was completely exhausted both in body and mind. With Pearl Harbor still in sight I was crying, too.

"Let's try once more," I finally said.

It was no use. Everything had been damaged.

"The devil!" I shouted.

I saw Diamond Head on my left. I set the ship toward our rendezvous point, Lanai Island, and collapsed. I fell into a deep sleep.

Near midnight I woke from my sleep. I felt some strength. After a while my aide fell asleep, perhaps unconscious. The ship had sailed all night in the moonlight with the hatch wide open.

When the dawn came I wondered where we were

going. Were we headed for our destination? Would we die before we got there? That was, however, only a moment's thought. Actually I had no energy to think about the future. I merely let the present continue. I did not wake my aide. I was dejected and defeated. There was nothing to say.

A little later I saw a small island on the horizon. I thought at once that we were coming to Lanai Island. O, heaven had not abandoned us. "Good! We'll make it yet," I thought. "If we get there now, while it is still dim, we will be all right." Although the ship had lost most of its power, I still had hopes of returning to fight. I shook my aide. Both of us took our respective positions and tried to run the ship faster toward the island.

I turned the gear to "full speed," but the ship only vibrated for a moment and would not go. White smoke shot up from the batteries. They had discharged all their electricity. There was danger that the batteries might explode. We knew that an explosion was possible, but we did not fear it. Death was in front of our very eyes.

At that very moment we hit a coral reef again. This was the end. We immediately thought of the explosives we were carrying as a matter of self-destruction just in cases such as this. No matter what should happen, we could not let the midget submarine fall into the enemy's hands. The time to destroy the submarine had come. We made up our minds.

We set the fuse afire.

When we made sure that the fuse was burning, we came upon the deck. In front of us dark waves were roaring angrily. The land was about seven hundred feet away. The moon was sinking in the west, and the sky in the east was lighting up. In the dim sky above there was the sound of enemy planes. My body was soaked wet with the morning mist.

"I go now," I said, and I jumped.

My aide followed right behind me.

The water was cold. The waves were big. I could not move freely and I swallowed salt water.

One minute. Two minutes. No explosion. I began to worry about the ship. The midget submarine had to be destroyed. I wanted to go back, but there was no strength left in me. Neither my aide nor I could shout to each other. Strength gradually went out of me. Then I saw my aide no more. He was swallowed up by the giant waves. I lost consciousness.

*US Navy*

# 3. *Struggle for Life*

AN AMERICAN army sergeant was standing beside me[9]. How it happened I did not know exactly. I remembered the time when I was in high school playing football. I was knocked down unconscious. After awhile I stood up and started running, but my mind was completely blank. Standing on the sandy beach, I felt numb and spent, my mind as blank as that time on the playing field. I did not know what had happened.

I offered no resistance. I did as I was directed. I was put on an army truck and carried away. I fell asleep.

When I came to myself, I found that I was in a building. I was told that it was in Honolulu.

"You were found on the beach near the Kaneohe Naval Air Station," they said.

I realized that the spot was on the northern coast of Oahu Island. That meant that we had driven the crippled submarine more than fifty miles during the night in complete blindness.

---

[9] Sakamaki was captured by Corporal David Akui and Lieutenant Paul Plybon of the Hawaii National Guard. [Ed.]

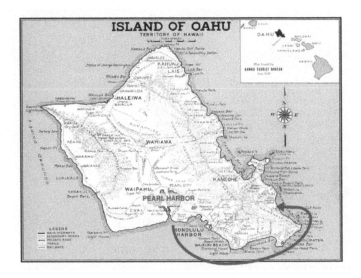

My mind went back to the scene of the attack.

All day on December 7, the enemy patrol ships were firing depth charges and seemed to be chasing the midget subs. I got the feeling somehow that my ship was the only real objective of those enemy actions and constantly watched the United States destroyers and constantly listened to every depth charge bursting in the water, for all these hostile moves seemed directed against me. From this I concluded that the other four midget subs had gone into the harbor while I was struggling with the destroyers.

Later I learned what had happened to them. One sub was sunk in the harbor. The second was sent to the bottom just outside the mouth of the harbor. Both of these craft were hauled out of the water later[10]. The

---

[10] Only one midget sub, I-22tou, was recovered approximately two weeks after the attack (see Appendix). [Ed.]

Japanese personnel found inside the subs were buried at Pearl Harbor with dignified military funerals[11]. That Captain Iwasa had been killed in action with one of those subs was clear from the shoulder insignia preserved by the United States Navy at Pearl Harbor.[12]

My guess about the remaining two was that one had been sunk by enemy fire and the other probably had never got started because of the trim not working as in my submarine[13]. I was sure that, as for myself, I could have achieved a spectacular success by firing the two torpedoes inside the harbor if my gyrocompass had worked normally so that I could navigate smoothly.

But, then, what was the use of such conjectures?

I had to face the grim reality about my own submarine, and the more I thought about it, the more terrible the thought became. The submarine whose mission and secret had been my life had simply failed to blow up as I had planned! It was captured just as I, its skipper, was. I was possessed by a terrible, uncontrollable shame. I trembled with the fear that through my fault the invaluable secret weapon had fallen into the enemy's hands. More than my own capture, the thought of the midget submarine's being made available to the enemy tortured my mind.

Whatever had happened to my submarine, however, there was nothing I could do about it any more. The

---

[11] There is no evidence of any military funerals for any submarine crews. [Ed.]

[12] Captain Iwasa commanded the submarine sunk by the USS Monaghan. [Ed.]

[13] All five submarines made it to the entrance to Pearl Harbor, at least one, maybe two, made it into the harbor. See Appendix. [Ed.]

only thing left for me was to plan what to do with myself. Die or live? That was the question. Yet, during the first two months I was detained on the island, I could not think anything vividly. I had no power of judgment. Even my memories of those days are vague, the only thing I do recall being several attempts to commit suicide. I failed in those attempts. Stripped of any means for killing myself, and my mind working only in a haze and in dark despair, nothing seemed to work. I simply cannot write anything intelligible about those days. My life was completely shattered. I was not myself.

My first clear recollection is the journey from Hawaii to the mainland of the United States. In the latter part of February, 1942, a group of three ships left the detention station. On two ships were Japanese and German nationals being shipped for internment on the mainland. On the third were American evacuees from Hawaii. I was confined in a room on this ship.

At the beginning of March I arrived in San Francisco. I stayed for one week at Angel Island in the harbor. Then I left from Oakland station for a long journey through the snow-covered Rockies, Salt Lake City, Denver, across the Mississippi, up into Minnesota, arriving at Camp McCoy[14], Wisconsin, on March 9.

The special train stopped alongside the camp. It was the end of the journey. The commanding officer and I walked at the head of a procession of German and Japanese internees through two rows of military police to the entrance of the camp. There was soft, dry snow under our feet.

The snow on the pine trees made me nostalgic. I thought of Japan, and my comrades in arms, and could not help wetting my eyes a little. The Japanese internees who had lived in Hawaii for twenty and thirty years were highly excited at the first sight of snow.

I was allowed to sleep in the same camp with other Japanese the first night. There were about thirty Japanese internees from California, Oregon, Washington, and Nebraska. It was the first time I met other

---

[14] Camp McCoy in Sparta, Wisconsin, became the largest holding facility for Japanese POW's on the US mainland. [Ed.]

Japanese face to face. They gave me words of comfort. I merely thanked them and did not say anything else. Germans in the next camp came to the fence and sent greetings to me. One of them who had been prisoner in World War I invited me for a walk. He, too, had been the skipper of a submarine. The next day I was removed to my own camp.

*Library of Congress, HABS*

Camp McCoy, Sparta, Wisconsin

An entirely new life had its beginning here. I had my bed in one corner of a mess hall. It was a leisurely and relatively free life.

For a while a German internee came and made hot water for my bath. When I found out that he was a volunteer, I begged him to stop. It was not because he was a German, but because I felt that I had no right to ask anyone to heat water for me. Then, when I thought about my comrades in arms fighting without the benefit of hot water baths, a comfortable bed and hot water bath seemed entirely too luxurious. Although the ground was covered with snow and the temperature

50

outdoors was several degrees below zero, I took cold-water showers just as I had always done in my service training period. It was good for my spirits as well as my muscles.

There was a stove in the room with plenty of coal beside it. But I would not go near it, let along use it.

"You are foolish," I was told. But I could not bring myself to see any use for it. To me there was no such thing as coldness or warmth.

Because I wore only a shirt and cotton suit, some of my Japanese neighbors sent me warm flannel pajamas, but I declined them. The commanding officer of the camp came one day with an interpreter and asked me,

"Do you need anything? Do you want anything?"

I shook my head.

"Then, do you need money?"

Again I shook my head.

"If there are things you would like to have, we will be glad to supply them for you."

"I do not have to have them, sir," I finally replied.

"But if I may have a pencil, a pencil sharpener, a notebook, some library books, and a daily paper, I should appreciate it very much."

The commanding officer seemed surprised.

"Don't you want anything like candy, cigarettes, or something to drink?"

I said, "When I think of the men at the battlefront, I cannot enjoy those things. My conscience does not allow me to have them. Thank you very much just the same,"

I was not being modest or deliberately hardheaded.

I simply could not enjoy them. That was how I had been trained.

I think the guard thought I was crazy when I took my daily cold shower.

From the morning bugle until taps at night I busied myself with the newspaper, books, meditation, and walks. I had no idle moments. I did not feel lonely at all.

After the snow melted away, rabbits jumped around the camp. Sometimes big hailstones fell upon the young leaves and the roof over my head. These hailstones were so big that it seemed dangerous to be hit by them.

In the afternoon the prisoners and internees gathered at the canteen. They sang Japanese folk songs in nostalgic tones. Some of the songs were those that we had sung on the ships in the navy. But to me at that time all songs were alike; they were merely songs just as all hills were hills to me. I had no esthetic or sentimental feelings.

The newspaper of April 9, 1942, reported the fall of Bataan. The newspaper reported it one way. That afternoon the Japanese at the canteen talked about it in quite another way. They seemed intoxicated with delight. I was not happy. A civilian psychology seemed so different from ours. We would not have rejoiced so lightly at an event like this. Every victory was a grim affair. It was a matter of life and death to us and the Americans. When people rejoiced so much over a victory, they became overconfident. This would lead to defeat, I thought. It was a deadly error to exaggerate every little victory or defeat. People who were not part of the actual combat often made that error. We had to work and prepare for all possible situations.

I was somewhat surprised that news of a defeat was printed on the front page. There was criticism of the government's conduct of war. There was no doubt, however, that the people and the government were firmly united in a resolve to wage the war to final victory. I prayed for a Japanese victory. I prayed for the success of my comrades.

On April 18 I read about the raid on Tokyo[15]. The news was like a stab in my chest. I was shocked. I felt that this was the beginning of real war. There was news of General Yamashita's great victory in Singapore and the account of a victory lantern parade in Tokyo. I was in the United States. America was no longer a country on a map. I was living there. I knew something of her resources. I could see the technological superiority of this country. I thought about the victory parade in Japan and wondered if the people were becoming relaxed and overconfident. I was in the United States. I saw things that told me that there was no easy road ahead for Japan. I was concerned... the raid on Tokyo. Real fighting was yet to come.

Corregidor was our victory. But the battle of the Coral Sea was America's.

I was all for Japan. Nothing in the world could change that. The only thing that seemed so unrealistic was the kindness of the American officers with whom

---

[15] Lt. Col. Jimmy Doolittle's daring B-25 bomber raid on Tokyo. [Ed.]

I came in contact.

The commanding officer of the camp was Lt. Colonel Harold I. Rogers[16]. He was generous and kind. He took care of me very well. He seemed to have a real understanding of us. Every morning he brought me a newspaper personally.

I saluted him and said, "Good morning, Colonel."

He was courteous and returned my salute with, "Good morning, Lieutenant." I was an ensign in the navy, but I supposed that he thought I ranked as a lieutenant in the army.

The colonel handed me the paper through the fence.

The chief engineer was Lt. Colonel H.E. Fillinger who had been to Japan. He told me of his impressions of Japan and he talked about American Indians whom he knew. I listened to him with interest, though not saying anything. There were other officers and enlisted personnel. They did not speak to me. I did not speak to them. Occasionally we "talked" by writing out messages on paper.

Perhaps the fact that I had not spoken a word except "Good morning, Colonel" may have aroused suspicion that I was slightly out of my mind. So I was not surprised when one day a medical officer came to see me. He was accompanied by an interpreter. He examined me and left without saying anything.

Whether I was normal or not was a matter of opinion. I know I was not normal to the American eye.

From the day I left civilian life and entered the

---

[16] He probably means Lt. Col. Horace I. Rogers., the officer in charge of Fort McCoy's POW camp operations. [Ed.]

seclusion of the Naval Academy, every moment of my entire life was devoted to strict conditioning of both my mind and body. The process not only had resulted in my losing sensitivity to the temperature changes in the atmosphere I breathed, but in complete separation from understanding of other human beings except those of my own kind in the services. The most curious thing that happened since my captivity, therefore, was a gradual awakening of my spiritual eye to the humanness of the Americans I came in contact with. This awakening came to me like a still small voice, so faint at first that I could hardly perceive it. But the tremendous effect of this new sensation was no less than the power that had steered me from a thought of suicide to a desire for life.

I cannot recall exactly when this transition to a desire to live took place. But when I became conscioius of it, the realization was like a sudden stab in my chest by a sharp knife. It was a stab against me, but it was more than that. It was a powerful hammer-blow against the heart of my whole past, the past that represented the entire history and culture of Japan out of which I, Kazuo Sakamaki, had been born and created. This was in reality the rebirth of reason. Reason! Where did I have it? Where inside of me had it been until then?

I searched and found it. I found it in those hills which I had earlier called mere hills. Those hills brought back the memory of my childhood. And in the young child that I was back at home, I found a human being and a human heart and a human mind. I remembered now. It was early summer. The hillside I saw from the window of my house was covered with a green carpet. Look! This very valley of Wisconsin was just like that scene of my childhood! Look at that setting sun! This was just like my home! My home! I was a human being once!

Could I ever go back there? Could I ever become a part of that nature? Could I ever become a human being again?

I fell upon my knees and, forgetting myself, began to pray. My reason was with me.

The leaves on the branches grew large. The air was full of early summer fragrance. The sunset was red and beautiful. I began to feel the difference between cold and warmth in the temperature.

I had to leave this camp in Wisconsin in the latter part of May, 1942. This was an important place for me. I will never forget it. I will never forget Colonel Rogers.

Two hundred and fifty Japanese internees left McCoy on the train that took us to Chicago. Then from Chicago, through the vast plains of Illinois, the train carried us southward and I fell asleep. When I woke up, the train was speeding through the green fields of Kentucky. I remembered that Abraham Lincoln had been born in one of those farmhouses in Kentucky. We entered Tennessee and crossed the Tennessee River winding through the Alleghenies, and I remembered the TVA. When the sun was shining against the hills, we arrived at a town that made me think of a fort city of Europe. It was Nashville. The train I was on was carrying some American troops. Members of a service organization came along and gave refreshments to the soldiers. This struck me as strange. They wore white aprons over their dresses and they handed out fruit, picture cards, and candies. They called, "Hi, soldiers," and seemed very friendly. As I was with the soldiers, I received a bag of candies myself.

There were young ladies and some old. But the majority were middle-aged. They looked neat and simple. They were sincere and kind. They seemed really interested in giving the soldiers comfort. I wondered if the women of Japan would realize that the women of America were not all like the female characters in a Hollywood movie.

When we arrived at the new camp, I saw five Japanese who had been brought in from the warm state of Florida. They told us of their life in America. I just listened to them without saying anything. I turned on the radio in the recreation room. The announcer said that a Japanese submarine skipper had just arrived in the camp. I did not feel good. I went to my hut.

A Japanese internee came and cleaned my hut.

"Please don't do it," I said. "Give me that broom." I did not want anyone to do my job. I was grateful for the kindness of other Japanese, but I could not accept it.

The camp was covered with tall oak trees. But the sun was strong, and the rays that came through the branches of the oak trees were scorching hot. It was like midsummer in southern Japan. Our main amusement was the squirrels that visited us every day.

Every afternoon clouds rose in the direction of Oklahoma, and there was a terrific shower.

In this camp there were six rows of huts. Each hut accommodated five or six persons. As I lived in one of those huts, for the first time since my capture I associated with other Japanese.

US Air Force

Camp Forrest, Tullahoma, Tennessee

There were some Italians. There were gay Italians and melancholy Italians. Some of them lived day to day just waiting for an exchange ship. Others spoke to me. I was struck by the sight of hairy men walking in pants. They whistled tunes as they walked.

The Japanese internees held classes every day: English, geography, agriculture, Buddhism, and theology. I attended every one of them.

There was news-broadcasting in the evenings. I learned that midget submarines had attacked Sydney, that there was some fighting off Madagascar, and also that there were fierce engagements in the Aleutians and at Midway. In that Midway battle the newspaper reported that the air struggle was particularly fierce. The Japanese secret code had been broken, I heard.

The United States was getting ready for a showdown fight. Damaged warships were repaired at Pearl Harbor and sent into service. The U.S. air force had concentrated its striking power at Midway. Large air reinforcements had been flown there. They were ready for a Japanese attack by the surface ships. To try to fight airplanes was suicidal for warships. A blind man did not fear a snake.

What I feared came true. The battle of Midway began. It was fought in the air. I knew what an aircraft carrier could do. Already the American forces knew by the use of carrier-based patrol planes where the Japanese ships were. They could tell every step of the approaching Japanese.

The fighter planes from both sides met. From the beginning to the end it was an air battle. I thought perhaps the two sides were well matched. But the result was a disastrous Japanese defeat. Perhaps the broken code was fatal to the Japanese side.

I saw a movie at this camp for the first time since the war. Deanna Durbin played the leading role. The film had been provided by the USO.

There was a great excitement at the camp one day when the group being repatriated left.

Some well-meaning friends asked. "What shall we report to the navy when we get back?"

I said nothing.

I saw them off in silence as they marched out from the gate of the camp. My life at Camp Forest came to an end.

Next I was moved to Camp Livingston, Louisiana.

When I arrived at this camp, the work on the site had

not yet been completed. Soldiers stationed here were going through a training for jungle warfare in the South Pacific. I was met by Japanese civilian internees. It was a very hot day. Most of them were residents of the United States, but there were some who had been brought in from South and Central America, mostly from Panama. They spoke Spanish among themselves, and except for their racial appearance they did not have much in common with the rest. Many of them were young men. There were altogether about 1,250 of us. I was housed in a separate hut near the entrance of the camp. Next to my hut was the hall for visitors. Families of Japanese internees came by train and automobile, some of them traveling more than two thousand miles.

Camp Livingston, Rapides Parish, Louisiana

The commander of the internee camp was Lt. Colonel Dan. He allowed me, without a guard, to spend the daytime with the civilian internees.

Mr. Fisher, a Y.M.C.A. secretary, visited me and talked to me alone. Although I understood him only in part, it was enough to give me additional assurance that there were people in the world who cared even for me. What influence those kindhearted individuals had upon my life cannot be adequately measured or told. I can only say that those human touches had begun to work on me with strange power. If anyone had tried to change me or my mind – if, indeed, any American army officer or religious worker had shown the slightest sign of trying to "convert" me – I am sure that, being in the mental condition I was in, I would have reacted with extreme skepticism. In fact I would have rigidly closed my mind. But they used no verbal propaganda. They did not try to tell me I or even Japan was wrong. They only wanted me to know and feel that in their minds I was human.

The Japanese had an "Internment University" and lectures were held in English, geography, penmanship, painting, sculpture, commerce, economics, agriculture, music, Japanese poetry, jujitsu, Japanese dancing, Buddhist scriptures, and theology. The chief of the educational activities was the Reverend Kano, a Japanese Episcopal clergyman from Nebraska. The "faculty" men under him were mostly professionally trained teachers and artists. The students were twenty years of age and older. Some students were as much as seventy years old. It was a thrilling experience to see these elderly men go to school with younger persons. I wanted my folks back home to see this. In Japan people at that age would merely retire into respectable uselessness.

The battle of Guadalcanal began. It seemed that the United States had started an offensive in real earnest. The war had entered a white-hot stage.

In September I moved to a corner of Area H in the

camp. I spent most of my time studying. From the newspapers I learned that some Japanese soldiers had been captured. Now I knew I had company. I watched the activities of these Japanese civilian internees. Their orderly life, well administered, was a constant source of inspiration to me. I had a lot to learn from these people who had spent most of their adult life in the United States.

One day in November when I was attending a class of the Internment University a guard came and said:

"You are going over to another area to be with other combat prisoners."

I thanked the Japanese friends who had taught me so much and left the area.

I met fifty new prisoners. There were from patrol ships that had covered Wake Island, patrol ships that had met the carrier from which the planes of the Tokyo raid of April 18 took off, and from submarines that had taken part in the Aleutian campaign. There were also prisoners from the battle of Midway. Commander Nakamune was the ranking officer among them. I heard the latest news of Japan from them.

I was at once given the job of gathering news for the new arrivals who did not know quite what was going on.

On January 1, 1943, however, sixteen prisoners led by Commander Nakamune left for another camp, leaving me in charge of the remaining thirty-six men! This was a tremendous responsibility, for the new prisoners were not as "tamed" as the civilians. They sometimes showed signs of hostility toward the

Americans. I wanted to prevent incidents by providing positive activities.

I called the entire camp to a meeting. I declared my policy, announced rules and regulations of the camp, organized the camp into groups, set up a daily schedule, and founded evening classes. I wanted to build a wholesome camp atmosphere by making possible full exercise of mind, heart, and hands.

Inactivity bred melancholia. Idle men imagined scenes of battle. Their status as prisoners of war made them, as Japanese soldiers and sailors, feel ashamed and dejected. I called them to the study hall and taught them American geography, American affairs, the fundamentals of English, mathematics, Japanese, and Chinese. I tried to lead them to live a peaceful life without depressing worries. I encouraged all kinds of recreation: softball, ping-pong, basketball, tennis. On Sundays we played softball with the civilians. We also worked to beautify our area.

Some complained that we lacked discipline – life was too free. Strong-armed men bossed too much. I tried to improve conditions by education.

In February, 1943, a group of ten prisoners led by Lt. Commander Matsumoto arrived from the Solomons. The sixteen who had gone west came back, without Commander Nakamune who had become insane. I turned over the leadership to Lt. Commander Matsumoto and looked after the noncommissioned officers. The arrival of these men told eloquently how the war was going.

At the beginning of 1943 Colonel Dan was replaced

by Colonel Weaver. Colonel Weaver told us one day:

"My brother was a lieutenant of the United States Navy. He was with the cruiser *Astoria*. You recall that when your ambassador, Mr. Saito, died, the cruiser took the body of the ambassador to Japan. My brother received fine treatment from the Japanese people. He was always saying good things about the land of cherry blossoms. Then, when this war came, both he and the *Astoria* were sunk by the Japanese. I cannot like the Japan that caused the death of my brother, but I would not forget the things he said about your country and people. You can rest assured that I will do my duty as the commander of this camp to the best of my ability."

It was said in a very friendly, though not undignified, manner.

The short winter was soon over. Then spring came. One day in May – it was a hot day – the order was delivered to us to go north to Camp McCoy, the camp where I spent my first months in the United States. I assembled the men and talked to them about Camp McCoy. I told them how the Geneva Convention concerning war prisoners worked.

When I came back to Camp McCoy, there were many Nisei[17] soldiers in training who later fought in Italy. This was the same camp that I had lived in before, and yet how many different things I noticed the second time. I saw robins, blue jays, and sparrows in the branches of the pine trees. Deer and pheasants from the nearby forests often strayed into our camp. When

---

[17] A person born in the US or Canada whose parents were immigrants from Japan. [Ed.]

rabbits and gophers jumped inside, we had a good time chasing them.

We were welcomed by friendly Colonel Rogers. According to the Geneva regulations we were assigned to some labor. We were well organized and well disciplined. The colonel seemed pleased with us. He tried to make us feel at home and human. His words and deeds helped us forget that we were prisoners of war. Sometimes for our amusement and recreation we were allowed to hunt small birds in the woods. We also made small huts for pigeons, pheasants, and, later, rabbits.

We planted vegetables in our own gardens: potatoes, cabbage, radishes, eggplants, melons, watermelons, beans, and spinach. When these vegetables appeared on our tables, the men were very happy.

After our arrival a recreation-and-work room was set up with a laundry machine, a sewing machine, and an electric iron.

It was just about this time that the midget submarine I had left behind was taken around the country to spur the War Bond Drive. It came to a town not far from the camp. I realized that through my error the submarine was now performing a strange duty: instead of sinking a warship, it was raising money with which to fight against Japan. The stranger thing was that I did not take it too hard. I knew then how much I had really changed.

The war situation was increasingly unfavorable for Japan, and Americans brought in additional prisoners who were desperate men. In September, 1943, thirty men were brought in from Attu Island. At the end of

1943 groups of ten and twenty, some of them suffering from malaria, came in. They were soldiers, sailors, and civilians. By the first of 1944 the total reached one hundred. Tarawa and the Marshall Islands sent another hundred. Thus in April there were more than two hundred Japanese prisoners. The camp was too small to accommodate them all. Officers were segregated and housed in one section of the infirmary.

Colonel Rogers said to us one day:

"I hear that you feel that you are fated to die. Some of you told us that your plight is desperate. Others among you petitioned us to recognize your customs and traditional ideas about being prisoners of the enemy. I understand all that. But please remember that a Japanese who was once a prisoner of the enemy later became a minister of the state. So why don't you relax and forget your ideas about being prisoners."

Colonel Roger's reference to a minister was about a man who played a prominent role in the Meiji Restoration. True, he was a prisoner once, but the "enemy" was a rival faction in a civil war. We were not able to feel very relaxed as Colonel Rogers suggested. The psychology of the men in our camp was radically different and tense.

The exchange ship brought tea and vitamin pills from Japan. The American Red Cross received them and gave us some of them. We were very grateful. The green tea made us homesick. The vitamin pills served to ease our nerves.

In spite of the mental suffering of the new prisoners, our camp life was relatively peaceful. It was well organized and there was unity. We did our work efficiently. The new arrivals were surprised and said:

"This camp life is better run than the army life in Japan. The harmony between the superiors and subordinates is very well maintained. To tell you the honest truth, we first thought that you were behaving so well because you were afraid of the Americans. But after a few days we found out that you do everything voluntarily. This is not a military life. This is more like a spiritual training camp."

I attribute this to the environment entirely. No wonder Commander Matsumoto used to say, "This is really a wonderful training. I must get as much as possible out of this life."

Saipan in the Pacific and Normandy in Europe were twin engagements whose outcomes would decide the future of the global war. We were sensitive to the events outside the camp. Then Italy surrendered. This caused us to sink markedly in morale. The invasion of Normandy was accomplished. Saipan fell to the American forces.

After the fall of Saipan our camp population jumped at once to more than a thousand! Alas! The war had now turned into a rout for Japan! Before I recovered from the shock, the cabinets changed in Japan. The road went downward steadily from then on.

What could I do? If I stared at the little flowers among the weeds, they were only white little flowers. If I looked at the wall of the infirmary, the color remained creamy white. Everything seemed to say to me, "You are only one individual. There is nothing you can do about it."

I turned my mind more and more to philosophy. Although my knowledge of English was inadequate, I read English books in order to find out more about the world, science, and life itself.

What change, however, had come over me! I compared "the present" with the time when I was alone in this camp. I was struggling with the problem of life and death. Now it seemed that even in this life as a prisoner of war, there was something new to learn every day, and instead of suffering from my own problems I was now teaching others! I had more reasoning power than I had ever had. I felt confidant. I felt a responsibility to lead others. I got ready for more prisoners to come.

On February 4, 1945, two hundred officers and men arrived from the Marianas. Lt. Commander Narita became our new leader.

One day Lt. Colonel Fillinger came to see us. He was doing everything possible as an engineer to make our life comfortable, which made us very grateful. He said, in an obvious effort to comfort us:

"Saipan fell. The Philippine Islands are reconquered. Now the Okinawa campaign is coming to an end. I know how all of you feel about your country. America's victory is now assured. So you see all of Japan is going to be our prisoner. It is not just you. There is no reason to feel ashamed. When it is all over, we will let you go. You will be happy, won't you?"

He meant well, but we were sad about the whole situation. We hoped that the kamikazes would do their job and somehow turn the tide.

We were moved again. This time we were brought to Camp Kennedy[18] in Texas. There were rows of small huts. This camp had been built since the war. There were many trees. As soon as we unloaded our luggage and looked around, we knew from the way the gardens had been taken care of that Japanese internees lived here before.

From the Marianas and Iwo Jima sixty new prisoners arrived. Germany had surrendered. With that depressing fact in the background, we started our semitropical life in the new camp. Officers were segregated from conscripted men, giving me more leisure which I used for study. During July and August there were fifty more new arrivals.

*National Border Patrol Museum*

Entrance gate to Kenedy Alien Detention Camp

---

[18] Located near Kenedy, Texas, it was officially called the Kenedy Alien Detention Camp. [Ed.]

The war reached the final stage. We heard about the atomic bomb and the entry of Russia into the war. We were shocked and repentant. We were combatants, all. This meant that our country's defeat was our responsibility. We had fought and lost. We could not blame the heavens. We could not blame others. We could not complain. It was all our fault. It was we who were weak. It was we who were inadequate. It was we who were ignorant. There was nothing we could say. We could only apologize. We could only shed tears.

There were some who could not believe that Japan had lost the war. They rubbed their eyes, but the fact was inescapable. I said to myself, "We've lost the war. We must return and work in silence. We must rebuild our country with our own hands. That is the only way we can pay our debts."

Our daily routine of work and study went on as usual after the end of the war. We were resolved that when we returned to Japan we would lay the new foundation of a new Japan.

Thus on December 1, 1945, we left our Texas camp and started our long journey homeward. There were eight hundred of us on this trip.

When the new year dawned upon us I was on the Pacific Ocean, leaving four years of life as a prisoner behind me.

# 4. *On the Surface, Harmony*

THE life in the prisoner's camps was not as simple as I have just described it. There were endless internal conflicts among the men. But the most persistent and difficult problem was the rivalry and jealousy between army and navy personnel. In order to understand the tension day in and day out, it is necessary to relate the story in one continuous sequence and tell it apart from the chronology. I tell it here so that the reader may get a glimpse into the background of the interservice feud that played not too small a part in the making of history as far as Japan is concerned. The best and the only way to reveal this perpetual conflict is by narrating the development of a situation involving some leading personalities with whom we shared our life behind barbed wire.

I was introduced to about fifty new prisoners at Camp Livingston. They had just got off army trucks which brought them. They stood and stared at me curiously, some with real hostility. They all had heavy beards on their faces. Their appearance was grotesque, to put it simply. To them I was, no doubt, a picture of failure, more so than themselves because I was the first to fail. I stared back at them. Neither side said anything.

The men were assigned to their barracks. I did not feel like meeting any of them. But when I passed by an officers' barrack, an aggressive-looking tall man came out and said:

"You are Sakamaki-San, aren't you?"

He sounded rather cocky but invited me in.

When I entered, I saw an older man in a blue jacket. He was stout and seemed about forty-two years of age. He just stood there and looked me over. I felt chills running down my spine.

"Commander Nakamune," said the first officer.

I bowed.

There was another man. He was Ensign Kanda. The man who had invited me was Lieutenant Kajimoto.

Commander Nakamune was the leader of the fifty new prisoners. I learned that he had been the aircraft carrier *Hiryu's* chief engineer. When the carrier was sunk at Midway, he barely made a lifeboat. He drifted about the Pacific Ocean for fifteen days, half dead. He was picked up by an American warship.

Commander Nakamune had a wife and children in Japan. His oldest son was a student in the Tokyo Imperial University. Unlike other Japanese officers, he did not hide his affection and longing for his wife. This, however, damaged his dignity among the men, particularly among the army personnel.

One day the commander called me in and when we were along said in all seriousness:

"There is no telling what will happen to us here. We may have to die. I, for one, am ready for anything. I trust you are."

Then on the day when he and fifty other prisoners received an order to transfer to another camp in California, Commander Nakamune turned pale and shivered all over.

He said grimly:

"I don't think they are going to send *us* to California. I know where they are taking us. Washington, D.C.! You know what they are going to do to us there? They are going to torture us and hang us."

After this he was always attempting suicide and failing in it. He once cut his belly with a razor blade. He jumped from the beam.

One day he brought a baseball bat to me and said:

"Ensign Sakamaki, will you hit me with all your might?"

He bent down and patted the back of his bald head.

"Here. Hit me here with this."

I did not touch the bat.

"Kill me, kill me, I beg you," he asked seriously, coming close to me.

Seeing that I would not take the bat, he dropped it and sat facing me. He wrung his neck with his large hands and said:

"You are strong, Ensign. Just squeeze my neck for five minutes, then it will be all over. I just can't stand it. I want to end it all right now."

I refused to obey him.

Commander Nakamune had a curious but unique

method of self-torture. He had imagined that the United States government was operating a powerful wireless station in Washington, D.C., and that strong waves of electric ether were being aimed at all prisoners. Commander Nakamune supposed himself to be particularly receptive to those waves. According to his calculation, he was worth a hundred thousand volts of live electricity.

When he could not stand the ether wave, he took a bath. He was in the bath several times a day.

If the ether waves caught him out of his bath, he hurriedly covered his bald head with a wet towel. The towel was full of broken glass pieces which he thought prevented electricity from penetrating him.

When he had come to me with the bat, he complained that he had too much electricity inside him.

"They are sending it now. I am being overcharged with it. My heart is a condenser, and my stomach a reactor. I can't stand it! I can't stand it!"

The baseball bat was not an accident. He was a real baseball fan and not too bad at playing it either. He used to play first base and caught the ball I threw from third base almost professionally. Later, however, I had to take him off the line-up for a reason which I will explain soon.

When I refused to co-operate with him in his scheme of self-destruction, he started to cry.

He was worried about his family.

Whenever a new prisoner arrived, he grabbed him an asked:

"Do you know anything about my son?"

More than once he asked me the same question, and I gave him the same answer: "Don't worry. Your family thinks that you have died honorably." He believed it and smiled happily.

Then the electric waves would come. He would tremble and ask:

"Do you think my family is all right? The Americans are sending the electric waves all the way to Japan. America is very advanced technologically. Look what they have done to me already. I am half mechanized! You laugh, but you see, because I am a machine I can hear the message from Japan, too. My family is all right now. The waves are not so strong today."

I did not laugh. It was not so funny when I remembered that in my early days as a prisoner, my own head used to feel like this. I was nervous as the commander was. I was all nerves myself. Then my imagination controlled my thinking. Commander Nakamune was going through the same stage. The only question was, would he calm down someday?

I wanted to protect and help the commander. He was not only my superior in the navy, but another human being going through the same experience that I had gone through. I did everything I possibly could. I washed his dirty underwear. I kept my eyes on him constantly. But what I had feared finally came.

One day he was jumping around in the camp ground shouting madly. I rushed out and held him in my arms to calm him, but he was already out of his mind.

He was taken to the infirmary and stayed there permanently.

Lieutenant Kanda also went out of his mind. He ran wildly over the ground, calling his wife's name. He, too, was taken to the infirmary.

The loss of these two officers was a blow to us all. It was a terrible blow.

I took over the leadership from Commander Nakamune. Then one day came Lt. Commander Matsumoto. In deference to his superior rank I gave way to him. He was a much older person than Commander Nakamune. Despite his age, he was a bundle of energy. He had had an extraordinary career in the navy. In 1905, when he was eighteen, he took part in the famous naval engagement in the Japan Sea against the Russian fleet. He had spent forty years in active service. This fact commanded the respect of us lesser men. But he was arrogant and seemed quite ruthless. I feared that his leadership would create trouble. So when he said to me, "I am much too old to direct the camp life. You act as my deputy and do everything," I was frankly relieved. But what he meant was that I should do as he ordered. I did not mind it except that his methods did not promise to create harmony with the army personnel who, with the development of the war situations, seemed to grow in number.

Commander Matsumoto liked to make paper dolls, of all things. He was good at it, and it was known that the American commanding officer like them so well that he kept some dolls in his office. The American soldiers nicknamed Commander Matsumoto "Old Paper-doll Maker." But the young Japanese prisoners, particularly the army men, did not think too much of the old man's hobby.

Up to this point it was all a navy show. But with the succession of "undignified" activities of the naval officers, there seemed to have arisen a feeling among the ranks of the army officers and men that an opening wedge had been made.

No doubt looking for some excitement, several younger officers came to see the "Old Paper-doll Maker." They intended to ridicule him.

They said, "You make fine dolls, but dollmaking does not seem to be a hobby becoming an officer of the navy."

This was plainly asking for trouble. Commander Matsumoto pushed paper and paste aside and rose up deliberately. He stared at everyone and his breath came hot and his breathing fast. The room was charged with his wrath.

He roared, "Who do you think you are? I may be old, but I have not lost my sense of judgment. You are too young to know what I am doing this for. Now get out and mind your own business."

The commander had wanted to promote peaceful hobbies among the prisoners to keep them happy until he succeeded in bringing them safely home to Japan. But even to suggest that the warriors of Japan dreamed of returning home after being prisoners was considered to be an act of high treason. This was like admitting spy activities.

The recalcitrant younger men seized this as an opportunity and started a vicious rumor. "Anybody who is thinking of going home alive is not a Japanese soldier. Anybody who loves life so much is not a soldier." These behind-the-back talks were like calling Matsumoto a coward and cheat. Such accusations sound strange, but that was the old official ideology of the Japanese militarists. So the officers of lower ranks and of the army used it as an excuse to get rid of the old man as the leader.

Matsumoto and the commanding officer were very friendly, too. The commander often seemed over-anxious to please the American officer. This was unbecoming a Japanese soldier, the accusers said among themselves.

One evening the officers gave a welcome party for a few army officers who had just arrived from Guadalcanal. Ostensibly the occasion was for the promotion of friendly relations between the army and navy in captivity. Unfortunately, however, the old grudge pushed its head up as beer swells the heads of the men.

The commander opened up: "The camp looks harmonious on the surface, but underneath there is trouble."

One of the newcomers asked innocently, "What's wrong?"

"It's the problem of ranks, also the problem of work. The army is the trouble maker."

Lieutenant Sato of the army pretended not to hear it. The navy commander went on:

"Take, for instance, Ensign Sakamaki and Lieutenant Ooi. Both are graduates of the same year. But the ensign was captured earlier. So since the prison camp has no promotion, he stays an ensign, while a man who comes in later has had a chance for promotion. This is a typical case. So sometimes younger men, when they come here, find themselves superior in rank to older men. It goes to their heads.

"The trouble with work is that the conscripted men do physical labor and according to the Geneva Convention receive eighty cents a day. But the officers are not supposed to stoop so such work so they get ten cents a day. Some superiors must wash the inferior's underwear in order to earn spending money. Then the men who work in the vegetable gardens act as if they are feeding the officers."

Nothing happened at this party, but the issues had been clearly defined by the talkative commander.

The day after the emperor's birthday was the holiday of the Yasukuni Shrine – the shrine for the soldiers and sailors who died in the war. We held a service of prayer. But when the last incense was burned and everyone was ready to leave, Commander Matsumoto got up on the platform and shouted, "Wait, everyone!"

We held our breath in the atmosphere of tense silence. The commander began:

"We are living together here. If all of us adhere to the virtue of humility, there should be no cleavage between the army and navy. But there is someone among you who is stirring up trouble. He wants to fish in troubled water. I will identify him soon."

I looked around. Lieutenant Sato of the army was

grinning meaningfully and mysteriously.

Commander Matsumoto went on:

"You of the army may feel dissatisfied. You may feel that you are dominated by the navy here. But that is not true. If an army man with a higher rank than myself should arrive here, I will gladly give him the command of the camp. But until then I cannot and I will not tolerate anyone who connives to disobey my authority. Such a plotter will be exposed and punished severely."

He looked over the room, and when his eyes recognized Lieutenant Sato his eyes stopped as if frozen.

"Lieutenant Sato!" shouted the commander.

The room was electrified. The commander seemed unable to control himself any more. He gave a command in a hot short sentence.

"From now on, no one will be permitted to hold a meeting without my consent. Dismissed!"

The meeting broke up without incident. But when I went back to my room, I thought that something had to be done or that something would happen.

Something did happen. Commander Matsumoto had gone to the latrine after the meeting and slipped on the icy step. He fell hard and lost control of himself. A medical officer of the army looked at the semi-conscious man and declared, "Heart attack and some internal bleeding. Tonight will tell the story."

The commander officer of the camp was notified. Lt. Colonel Rogers came at once and looked after Matsumoto like an intimate friend in trouble.

The commander survived. So did the old trouble between the two services. But since Matsumoto was incapacitated, the leadership was transferred to a young army man, Lieutenant Kajimoto, who, like Commander Nakamune, was from Midway.

Lieutenant Kajimoto was a modest and serious man. He described his new job in these words, "Now I have the most difficult job in the whole army!"

It seemed that Kajimoto was thoroughly tired of everything and really anxious to call it a day any time. "But," he said, "it's not easy to die. Only, living is much more difficult."

A few days later a fierce fight broke out in the recreation room over the question of who was first at the pool table. It turned out that a younger army man with a higher rank demanded his turn over a navy man who was one year his senior in age. The two exchanged body blows and one of them was knocked down unconscious and wounded severely.

The next day the new leader called everyone. Appearing lifeless, Kajimoto announced his determination.

"We had a violent fight yesterday. Whether is was yesterday or not is not important. This camp is full of trouble. As we are forced to live together, we are apt to have trouble. Sometimes you feel like socking somebody. I was on a carrier off Midway. After the ship was sunk I drifted around fifteen days before I was captured. So I have no claim to an officer's rank. In a prisoner's camp all ranks are meaningless as far as rights are concerned. But until my rank is taken away from me by a courtmartial, I must perform my duties accordingly. I will not give you orders, but I would like to appeal to your reason. I have only one thing to say to you. If you make any more trouble, you will see me no more in this world."

That and the segregation of officers ended the trouble, for the time being.

# 5. *Talks on Suicide*

PERHAPS my brief chronology on the camps or the conflict between the army any navy is not particularly significant. If someone else had been captured on December 8, 1941, instead of me, he would have had good treatment and a gradual change of outlook on life as I had. The jealousy between the two branches of the service is not perhaps peculiarly Japanese.

There was one thing, however, which, I am rather sure, was unique with the Japanese prisoner of war. I cannot completely give an honest account of our camp experiences unless I go into the problem of the psychology of suicide which was ever present in any Japanese prisoner-of-war camp.

One night the clock on the infirmary struck two. Suddenly someone shouted, "Attack! Charge!"

It was Sergeant Ikawa. He was out of bed, jumping around. Someone hastened to him and hugged him.

"Sergeant! Sergeant Ikawa! This is an infirmary. Please calm yourself."

"What! You, Yamakawa? What are you waiting for?

It's my order. Attack. Private First Class Yamakawa, take over, and lead the attack. Hurry!"

Sergeant was back on Attu. He was wounded and in great pain.

"Sergeant Ikawa! This is Ensign Sakamaki," I said. "You will be all right soon. Please go to sleep."

"What? Something's wrong here. Who cut my leg? I have lost my leg. Hey, Yamakawa, bring me a hand grenade. You go ahead. I am going to blast the enemy and myself together."

Captain Pintozzi, the American medical officer in charge, came and asked:

"What's going on?"

Sergeant recognized it as English.

"I hear English. The enemy is here. The enemy is attacking. Come on, Yamakawa, attack!"

"Sergeant, Sergeant, this is Ensign Sakamaki. Commander Matsumoto is here, too. That was the captain. We are at Camp McCoy."

"Ohhhh, I'm hurt. Ensign Sakamaki? You say that was our medical captain? He? Oh, then it's all right. Thank you."

The captain gave him an injection of morphine, and the sergeant quieted down. Old Commander Matsumoto put the blanket over the sergeant.

I remembered about the sergeant. He was nearly frozen on Attu. He had not slept for several days. Finally he tried to blow himself up with a hand grenade. He did blow himself up partially, but only the bottom half of his body was blown off. He lay in the trench, asleep, half dead. A few days later, when the Americans were cleaning up the corpses they came upon the sergeant. They found his heart still beating. So they carried him out and put him on board a transport bound for Seattle.

"This ship is overcrowded, and he won't live anyway. We had better abandon him," someone suggested.

"No, we cannot give up a human being as long as his heart is beating. Put him in the operating room."

As the operation progressed, the sergeant began to regain his consciousness. He looked around and saw unfamiliar faces. With weak breath he murmured, "A-me-ri-ka! Oh... I'm a prisoner, then..."

Sergeant Ikawa lived – lived in the agony of being a prisoner.


Petty Officer Kawamoto came into my room. He was crying. I cried with him. Why I cried I could not explain. Kawamoto was crying because he was a prisoner and alive.

"Ensign Sakamaki, do you understand me? I was fighting against a cruiser. My sub was already crippled. But we fought and fought. Then we hit against something. Perhaps it was a collision with the enemy cruiser. Bang, bang, bang! The whole submarine shook and everything went wild. We began to sink. Then a depth charge hit us right in the middle. We were sinking fast...we did not want to go down like that. We floated by, filling all our main tanks with air. The enemy was right in front of us. Bullets came like hail. Something ripped through my leg, and I fell into the water.

Everything went black. Then I came to myself. Where do you think I was? I was on an operating table of the cruiser I was trying to sink!"

Water, water, everywhere. Far as one could see, it was nothing but a rolling blue field of salt water. Yesterday one comrade fell out dead. Today another dropped out. How many have we lost so far?

"Cheer up! We have come farther west of Midway now. The war is just beginning. Live, everyone. We'll fight yet."

The carrier was in flames and smoke. Then a torpedo hit her. She began to list. Everyone was trapped. Someone hammered his way out, and the other followed. A life raft was lowered. As soon as we got in it, the carrier went down. How many days since then have we been rowing? One by one, our comrades exhausted themselves and life went out of them.

"Comrades, comrades... You've fought well. We'll come and join you soon."

But we lost our senses. We did not see. We did not hear. We felt no more. We were dead. We could not even jump into the sea.

Several days later an American cruiser found us.

We had promised our comrades in arms, we had vowed to follow them, and yet we lived – as prisoners. Can you understand why we cannot live?

Every day in camp was like this. We were being tortured by our word of honor to our friends. *They* had given their lives, and *we* were living. They had died in the finest tradition of the fighting man, and we were living in the most contemptuous state – prisoners of the enemy.

We had come to this state of affairs not because we wanted to. At least in the early stages of war there was no voluntary surrender. Men of the navy had floated as long as possible. They became exhausted and had no strength to commit suicide or resist capture. Men of the army stayed in their positions for days and weeks without any supply of food or ammunition. They were either unconscious or too sick to know what was going on when they were taken.

Everyone of us was captured alive after we had fought furiously with all our might and mind. When we took the final step – a direct charge into an enemy position – we had fully expected to die in battle. Then something went wrong, and we were not killed. Worse still, we found ourselves in the hands of the enemy.

We cared not who the enemy was. The enemy was our opponent in battle. We had no hatred of the Americans as such. We only hated ourselves for failing in our duties and privileges. We hated our fate which had caused us to live after those death charges.

We were simple-minded fighting men. Though there were older men among us, some of us were celibates. We had no thought of carnal pleasures. We had been so trained that our thinking was all concentrated on the most effective means of expending our lives for a victory in war. Then we failed in the one thing we had lived for.

Then, when we realized that we lived, we thought about our parents, relatives, wives, children, and friends. They had no doubt buried us. We could imagine our funerals. We were heroes to them and to their neighbors. We were immortalized at the Yasukuni Shrine. The emperor had gone there to conduct a ceremony for us. Thousands of people bowed before our souls. Our names had been published. Our relatives received medals and citations. Someone urged the people, "Follow these men, the finest of all. Our country stands invincible, thanks to these immortal spirits!"

How could we face our people again?

Death by suicide was the only logical solution to our predicament.

Suicide in a prison camp would not be as glorious an end as death in combat. We had forfeited that privilege when we were captured. But in death we could redeem ourselves to those comrades who had given their lives on the battlefield. It would be belated, but not too late. Death in any form or by any means was better than failure to pay our debt to the country by living. We therefore considered our own individual ways of committing suicide.

Our desire for suicide, however, was thwarted on every hand. We had no knives to cut our throats. We had no ropes to hang ourselves with. Some of us banged our heads against every object in sight, and yet we did not die. Some men refused to eat. But the idea of dying slowly was even more trying than living hungrily.

Our life was one of dilemma. We wanted to die and yet we could not die. We wanted to kill ourselves and we could not. The dilemma had a decidedly deteriorating influence upon us. Under this dilemma everyone lost all surface dignity and pretense and became human with human problems, behaving like a human with many acute problems. This process was often sudden and crude. It exposed how much of our behavior under "normal" conditions was "put on" and how easily it peeled off.

When we were stripped naked behind the barbed wire, we were compelled to look at ourselves as we truly were – a picture of failure.

"But it was not entirely our fault," we said. "Fate has had something to do with it."

We had no hope for the future. We were at the very bottom of life. We despised ourselves. We were in a perpetual state of spiritual shock as prisoners of war. Death demanded our allegiance and yet life claimed our bodies. Images of past combat experiences kept coming back. The future was utterly bleak.

Strong-bodied men went out of their minds.

The fact that they were Japanese and prisoners at the same time and in the same person had made them insane.

Like sick people recovering in a hospital under the best of care, we, the prisoners, well protected and well fed, given excellent medical treatment in case of illness, became healthier in body. But our mental reaction to our past and present expressed itself in a cocky arrogance toward officers of higher rank who to us symbolized oppression and regimentation in the past. Sometimes we disregarded all rules completely and acted as if we were animals.

Not all of us, of course, were affected like this by the life of captivity. In fact, when new prisoners arrived in our camp, there were actually two distinct groups of men: one trying to maintain some order and reason, the other just the opposite. We old-timers extended them a warm welcome to assure them that life in camp was an experience in rehabilitation.

Our camp was run in accordance with the provisions of the Geneva Convention. The camp was equipped with every necessity. The American authorities were not only efficient as administrators, but sympathetic as overseers of our recovery. We on our part recognized our dependence upon our captors and co-operated with them, obeying their orders and endeavoring to build our camp in an orderly manner.

I made a speech every time we received new arrivals, which will indicate the line of thinking and behavior I felt was necessary for me to suggest to the new prisoners. This is what I usually said:

"You have fought bravely at the front and you were willing to give your life itself. I express my deep respect and appreciation.

"Now you and I are in the same situation. We are bound by the same fate. I can understand perfectly how you feel inside yourself. My sympathy for you has no reservations.

"However, since you have just arrived to start a new life with us in a co-operatively organized community, we would ask you to respect the regulations we have set up and to lead the kind of life you would not be ashamed of as a Japanese. This is a co-operative life, not a regimented life. If you have anything to say, no one is going to stop you. Please do not speak behind anyone's back. Bring it out into the open through the proper channels.

"How do we live here? What is our philosophy? I shall now explain it. First, if you stand in front of a mirror, what do you see? A human being. This is our starting point. Second, what does being human mean? It means that we are capable of organized social existence. We can and should act like members of human society. Third, we are prisoners of war. The United States government is our protector. We must abide by laws and regulations pertaining to the prisoner of war. I know how trying it will be for you to be a prisoner, but for your own sake I advise you to restrain yourself no matter how hard you find it.

"Fourth, we are all combatants once. We dealt in the business of destruction and death. But this camp is not a battlefield. I must emphasize that. I know that since your capture you have attempted more than once, at least in your mind, to take your life into your own hands. But you are now a prisoner, not a combatant, and your life is governed not by the lawlessness of war but by an international agreement. If you have come with any idea of yourself still being a soldier, abandon that idea at once. You are not a combatant any more. You are about to being a life as a civilized, organized, and cultivated person, fit to receive the benefits of international law.

"Fifth, we are not living here in isolation. The eyes of the world are upon us. What Americans think of us as they watch our daily conduct will have a far-reaching bearing upon all Japanese. If we look untidy and behave noisily, they will think us uncivilized. Some Japanese civilians will be repatriated to Japan. They will report to our relatives. If our unbecoming conduct should reach their ears, we shall disgrace them and can never redeem ourselves to them who have died for us. Even if we commit hara-kari, it would not be enough. However we must not live for the sake of what others may think of us. We must so live that we shall not be ashamed of ourselves.

"Sixth, let us consider the question of death. I refer to death by suicide. I contemplated it long before you did. It is imperative that we face this problem and think it through. No matter how much you may mourn over the uniform of a prisoner of war you are wearing, you cannot change the uniform. We do not like even to mention the words "prisoner of war." We hate to be looked at. We do not want anyone to know it. But that is sheer vanity. The letters P.O.W. on our backs will not depress us so much if we will think objectively. We are prisoners of war. We cannot be anything else right now. If you will adjust your thinking to the status of a prisoner of war, you will not have to struggle so much. Your names are known to the Japanese government through the Swiss government. That you are prisoners of war is now public information. Death or any other escape method will not alter the fact that you were once a prisoner. There is no use mourning over it.

"I know how much you want to hold someone else responsible for your present condition, but whom can you so hold? Do not try to connect your present misery with someone else's shortcomings. That you are here is your own fate. It is the way the heavens have seen fit to treat you. Be a man. Be a human being. Return to your true self and rethink.

"Suppose you have decided to hang yourself, or fight the guard and be killed, or steal a knife from the kitchen and cut your throat. What will the people of the world think of you? You yourself may think that you have done your duty, but the people of other countries will not understand why you have killed yourself so many days after your capture. They will not think you brave or praise you for committing suicide. They will write about it in papers and laugh about it. You who have seen America, even a little bit, should certainly be able to understand what I am saying.

"We are men. We regret that we missed our chance for death at the front. But dying on the battlefield is not the only honorable way to die. To complete our duties as men and live until our natural death is another manly way. We should, therefore, resist every temptation to weaken.

"If you had wanted to die, you should have died before coming here. You missed your last chance to commit suicide. You and I are now prisoners recognized as such by governments. There is no more honor or freedom for suicide. A suicide in the camp will only cause trouble for others.

"When we forget our small selves and return to reason, we will realize that the very fact that we have survived so far may reveal some unfamiliar things to us to do. This means that our capture is equal to our rebirth. We are born again. To live in humiliation as a prisoner of war may be more difficult than taking our own life, but it is our solemn obligation to live this renewed life as men.

"All of us who have preceded you here have gone through the same stage. We have attained a stated of mental resignation, thus enabling us to study and meditate. We have learned to believe that our future is in the hands of fate. We can follow our example and live beyond death. Do not use such a word as death any more. As long as you are here with us, leave the matter of your life and death to your leader. Please do not handle your life by yourself.

"A person's true mettle shows itself in crisis. How you handle yourself when you have had a serious failure is what is all important. Instead of letting your past torture you, build your future upon your failure. Often a misery has a way of turning into a blessing.

"Wash away your past and join our organized life as an integral member of it.

"According to the tradition of Japan, to be a prisoner is to be a traitor. But to worry about it now is a waste of time. You will only expose your vanity. You died with your past. Now you must live anew.

"You may say that the people back home would not understand you unless you committed suicide. They may not understand it now, but heaven does. There was a man with us at another camp. He was a Mr. Nago of Hawaii. He was captured in the Russo-Japanese War. He was not welcomed by some villagers when he returned home and came to Hawaii. I know that he has led a life of singularly high quality. You may be likewise rejected by your people, but that is not the end of you.

"Once we were not afraid of anything. We are here because of war. It is our fate. We should not listen to any human criticism. I cannot tell you how long this stigma will follow us, but as long as we do nothing shameful before heaven, we have nothing to fear from the tradition or custom.

"As long as we breathe, we are living as human beings. Let us, therefore, spend all our time improving ourselves as humans. You may not have future or hope for future now, but you can live each day as fully as humanly possible. I am not saying that this will be easy. I know that when you open a book, you think of war; when you hold a pencil, you think of war; and when you go to bed, you think of war. You cannot wipe out war from your minds right away. But look at your new friends here. They have been at the business of being a prisoner longer than you have. What are they doing now? They are alive today because they live one day at a time; they live today's life today. Don't live today in yesterday.

"Let us not therefore talk about the past. Let us concentrate on what we must do today. If you will occupy your mind with the task for the day, you will have no time for the past. We have a lot of healthy and enjoyable work to do. We have many facilities for recreation. Let us make this camp a happy place to live in.

"It is said that idleness breeds mischief. Leisure-time activities are an important element in our camp life. You can do almost anything here: painting, calligraphy, sculpture, animal husbandry, gardening, carpentry, sewing, reading, writing. If there is something else you want to do and you need something we do not have, I will try to get it for you. We have a daily paper, some magazines, and a radio. Look around in the library. If you will read all the books there – there are some Japanese books, too – you will have no idle moments. The army, the Y.M.C.A., and the Red Cross, all the agencies rendering service to prisoners of war, will give us assistance if we need it.

"In order to live happily here, we must first get intimately acquainted with one another. We need mutual understanding. I know the difficulty involved in what I have just suggested. Among as are army men and navy men, combatants and civilians, superiors and inferiors in age and rank. Sometimes your inferiors in age or rank may have to lead you. The important thing is to respect the dignity of the other person regardless of his rank or age. When we have genuine mutual respect, there will be real harmony among us. The old rivalry between the army and navy, between the military and civilians must go. This is no place for petty competition. Harmony through helpfulness to others is the key to any social life.

"You are young yet. If youth should lose youthfulness, what good is it? While you are young, it is the time to train yourself, polish yourself. A prison is a good school for life. To live here is a study in life.

"You do your part and you cultivate your mind. Do your duty and be diligent. Only as each one does his task is an organized life possible. A useful motto to bear in mind is to mind your own business. Let us not trouble ourselves with finding fault of others. A person may do thirty wrongs and seventy good things. Give him credit for the good he does.

"If you don't know which way to turn, pause and refresh yourself. When you meditate, the light will come your way. Do not let evil possess you. Overcome it with justice within yourself.

"Time to reform yourself is now. The saying, 'Strike while the iron is hot,' applies to you today. I ask you, therefore, to renew yourself early in the camp life and you will forget yourself and live in the present. Make your heart pure, and bright will be your life.

"When you come in contact with American military personnel, you may first experience some unpleasantness. Bear it like a man. Their ways are different from ours. In our differences we may find something to learn. You can use this opportunity to learn something about America. Do not close your eyes. Observe the unfamiliar with an open mind, study and inquire. Judge and learn. That is the way to knowledge."

When I finished, there were tears in the eyes of the new prisoners. There was a sense of new resolve in the hearts of the men as they began a strange life in a strange land.

As a means of rehabilitation, we held many classes of study. But the problem of language was always troublesome. At Camp Kennedy, Texas, English was the only medium permitted.

"Why should we study English?" was a natural question. I had to make another speech. What I said, I think, tells what the men were thinking in those days.

I faced them and said:

"I am not unaware of the fact that English has been completely abolished as a subject-matter in the secondary school in Japan. I know how you feel – you are absolutely opposed to studying English or studying in English. I understand that there are some among you who pledged when captured never to speak a word of English.

"Since English was dropped by the Ministry of Education in Japan, you may say that studying it is an un-Japanese activity. I am Japanese. When I propose to you that you study, I do not do so without deep deliberations. I have thought of our own past, present, and future. I have considered the world situation, the plight of prisoners in general, and the ways of men, and the educational system of Japan. I have come to the conclusion that the study of English is necessary and desirable. I shall assume full responsibility for the use of English in our camp classes.

"Our individual national civilizations are largely built up in one language system. Peoples of the world have come to feel self-sufficient in their own languages. But does this help the cause of mankind? Look at our own history. At one time we had to import from China and Korea not only Buddhism but all branches of knowledge. Our ancestors took from China and Korea what was best in their civilizations. It was when Hideyoshi[19] and Iyeyasu[20] forbade Christianity and closed up the country that our civilization began to deteriorate. They assumed that the indigenous genius of Japan was sufficient. But they were wrong. The march of human progress overtook Japan. When the country was reopened in the middle of the nineteenth century, Western civilization rushed into Japan like a flood. The leaders of the new Japan knew that isolation from the rest of the world had greatly retarded Japan. How they sought knowledge in all the world is well known to you. Such pioneers as Joseph Neeshima[21] and Shoin Yoshida[22] went, or dared to go, abroad when leaving Japan was prohibited on the pain of death. But it was these men who first brought back to Japan all the virtues of Western civilization and helped advance the culture of Japan. We must likewise clear our minds of prejudice and be able to hear what others have to say. The way to advance our nation is to increase our knowledge of the world's civilizations and apply what is best in them to our lives. If Japan is to make progress she must adopt the strength of the West and make it vital. We must look all around us, sharpen our senses, build our mind and body, and use all the good things in

[19] Toyotomi Hideyoshi, war lord and dictator in the sixteenth century.

[20] Tokugawa Iyeyasu, successor to Hideyoshi, and the first of the Tokugawa's who ruled Japan until the Meiji Restoration, 1867.

[21] Joseph Neeshima, famous founder of Doshisha (Christian) University in Kyoto.

[22] Shoin Yoshida, a daring youth who attempted to escape from Japan to study abroad, was arrested and executed. His followers later succeeded and carried out Yoshida's wishes.

the world.

"I do not believe for a moment that Japan has reached a level of civilization equal to any in the world. Self-sufficiency is the first step in degeneration. Time never stops. Those of us who live in the twentieth century must live with the twentieth century.

"Although English has been abolished in the secondary school, I do not believe that it has been done away with in higher education. It is important to know our enemy in war. Similarly it is important to know others out of war. We know that blindness in combat is utterly stupid. Blindness anywhere is likewise so. In order then to understand others we must learn their languages. Knowing a foreign language is one sure way to open our eyes to the affairs of the world.

"I do not believe that learning English in your position as a prisoner of war makes you a traitor. After all you are in the United States. Everything that comes to you is in English. Every American with whom you come in contact speaks English. They have some surprisingly fine qualities that we can learn. This is an opportunity. The only thing we must be on guard against is profanity in language. We must reject negative things and at the same time accept the positive.

"As we are in daily contact with Americans, there are bound to be some difficulties between us, as we have had. The chief cause of them is the language barrier... If you have any trouble in the future, take the matter to your leader. But it would seem desirable if you understood and could attend to matters of daily routine. Reliance upon one's superiors all the time destroys one's initiative. I will tell you a story.

"One day an American guard brought a bucket to a Japanese soldier. The latter thought that the American wanted the room cleaned. So he tried to show by hands and gestures that he had cleaned it. The guard, also by gestures, ordered him to fill the bucket with water. So he filled it and then emptied it on the floor and started to sweep it. The American soldier immediately stopped it. The Japanese soldier got disgusted and threw the bucket away. The guard scolded him. Thereupon the two started a hot argument, one in Japanese and the other in English with an obvious result. I was called to straighten it out. What do you think the guard wanted? He had wanted the bucket kept filled all the time and placed near the stove to prevent the air in the room from becoming too dry and to serve as a fire-fighting apparatus also.

"You ate a good meal today. You know who cooked it? Sergeant Manabe. He comes from Midway. He had gone only to higher elementary education at home. When he was captured he knew only a few words in English. He realized that as a sergeant he still had some responsibility for his men. In order to do his job well under the Americans, he felt, he had to know enough English to run things smoothly. He never stopped learning and today he knows enough English to do our cooking for us. It is important for us that he understands what he is doing, don't you think?"

# 6. *From War to Peace in Japan*

THE repatriation ship approached the port of Uraga, of Commodore Perry's fame[23]. I saw Mt. Fuji, and I knew I was home.

After we got off the ship, we were assembled in a place where there were repatriates from other parts of the world. They all seemed restless and confused.

Port of Uraga, Japan

---

[23] Commodore Matthew C. Perry entered Uraga on July 8, 1853, in America's campaign of "gunboat diplomacy" to force Japan to open ports to American trade. [Ed.]

A Japanese official in charge of the repatriation told us:

"You need not feel ashamed. You don't have to worry about your status. Please work hard."

I went to the office to see the staff members. They said:

"We receive many repatriates every day. But somehow those who return from the United States are the best in appearance as well as in utterance. They are the calmest, too. Others are emotionally rather unstable. Some cry, some sing, others jump around like little children. But they are mostly incoherent."

"Thank you," I replied. "We are all anxious to start working to rebuild our country. To us our personal feelings are secondary. That is why we do not laugh or cry."

I completed all formalities of separation and said good-by to the others. We pledged ourselves to work for a rebirth of Japan.

The return of P.O.W. No. 1 was not without some news value. As soon as I reached home, several newspaper reporters surrounded me. A typical news story about me ran something like this:

"Ensign Sakamaki who took part in the Pearl Harbor attack with the other nine who died for their mission has come back after having spent four years in the United States as a prisoner of war. He was the first to be captured and so he was known as P.O.W. No. 1. He received good treatment in various camps in the United States. He arrived in Uraga on January 4. But when the reporters called on him at his home, he would not talk to anyone. His father expressed regrets that Ensign Sakamaki wished to remain silent for a time while he paid reverence to the victims of the war in humility."

I became a sort of public figure and an object of varied emotional reactions on the part of the public. Every day letters poured in. I quote from a few representative ones.

"Your past is not wrong at all," a correspondent wrote. "You need not feel ashamed. On the contrary, we owe you thanks. With a new heart, please work for the reconstruction of our beloved country."

A man who called himself a patriot said "No wonder we lost the war, Mr. P.O.W. No. 1. Although I am a mere merchant, I know how to commit hara-kiri. A man who does not know what shame is, is a beast. If you want to die now, I will gladly come and show you how it's done."

The "Worried About Japan" wrote, "Which is the more manly life – live long and cheap, or live short but glorious? Shame on you."

Some people wrote not only once, but twice and three times. Here is a typical repeater:

"I cannot understand how you could return alive. The souls of the brave comrades who fought with you and died must be crying now over what you have done. If you are not ashamed of yourself, please explain how come. And if you are ashamed of yourself now, you should commit suicide at once and apologize to the spirits of the heroes who died honorably."

These were all from men. In contrast to them, letters from women were very solicitous. The news that I was a bachelor had something to do with it. I shall talk about this in the next chapter.

The cities of Japan were of course in ruins beyond description. Enough has been written about this. The shortage of materials had already started a spiral of inflation without any effective check. Everyone has heard this, too. The discipline of wartime was relaxed and morality was low. Democracy tried to replace the old feudal order, and there was endless confusion. Human hearts were bitter.

But I found affection in abundance when I returned home. My folks were surprised to see me. I changed their surprise into joy, and together we changed that joy into a prayer of thanksgiving for the good treatment I had received in the camps in the United States. My friends and neighbors welcomed me.

I was eager to work. Many job offers came to me. But since I was "the talk of the town," I felt that I should choose my place and nature of work with utmost care.

I ruled out big cities first. I knew that there was a ban on immigration into congested areas. Besides such opportunities as were available were connected directly or indirectly with the abnormal economy of postwar scarcity. I wanted none of that.

The first real offer was from a newspaper company. A representative said, "You lived in the United States and understand democracy. Is it not your duty to interpret it as a newspaper writer?"

He was sincere and the offer had been made in good faith, but I could not accept it because I was not trained for it.

Former navy friends urged me to go into the lumber business. I declined this, too, because I did not feel that I could fit into a complicated and risky business organization.

Someone suggested that after the experiences such as I had had I should enter the religious field. "You have had a most unique career as a suicide skipper of a submarine. You must have developed an appropriate philosophy of life. Why don't you dedicate your life to the task of enlightening the people of Japan who are in the dark?"

I could not see myself in such a role because I was not religious.

There was another strong suggestion that I become a miner in a coal pit in Kyushu. This was out of the question because my farmer parents would not be able to accept the idea of their son digging underground.

I decided to work on the family farm and wait for a better opportunity.

When I braved the world and started to work on the farm, I overheard conversations of other farmers who were perhaps talking loud enough for me to hear.

"What has the world come to? No one can work wholeheartedly. We don't know what's going to happen next. We just can't put our minds into our work. What a foolish thing our ministers and generals have done! If it was obvious from the beginning that Japan would lose, why did they start it in the first place? I am so mad I cannot work."

Someone agreed. "What weaklings our soldiers

turned out to be! Sure, they said they were invincible and all that. But they lost everywhere and in the end they had the nerve to say and demand that we all fight the enemies in the homeland. But with what? Bamboo spears! I just can't help laughing. Do you know that we didn't have even enough airplanes or mechanized divisions? I cannot hate the militarists too much. It's their fault that we are having such a hard time today."

The people, however, did not mind the Americans a bit. A woman said, "Our leaders told us that if Americans came we would all be killed. But the Occupation soldiers are rather nice. Americans are different. There are many kind people among them."

A man who lost everything was naturally bitter. "What a stupid war this has been. I lost my children and my house because of it. If I knew that I was going to suffer so much, I should have died before."

Someone was happy. "This is really a new world all right. There is no longer any difference between the rich and the poor. Before, the militarists and government officials looked very important, but I don't think much of them now. When I think of the time when we were called dirty peasants and compare it with our importance today, I feel wonderful."

There were sincere efforts from the top to introduce many necessary reforms, one of which was thinking for oneself. But habit dies hard. The masses of people merely followed the crowd, or the leaders, to be more precise. Democracy was a new word and while there were individuals who sincerely wanted to understand it, the majority accepted the idea the same way they accepted militarism: "We cannot help it."

General MacArthur was supreme both in name and fact. Everything he said was taken with resignation. "We cannot help it." Pretty soon "MacArthur" became a common noun. If a housewife dominated and ruled over her husband, the people said, "Too bad, she is a macarthur."

By the first anniversary of the end of the war there was a new kind of realization. People realized that no one could help them but themselves. This increased selfishness on one hand, but on the other there was growing evidence that people worked harder. There was a new consciousness that the individual improvement had direct relationship with the recovery of Japan.

Though the general psychological atmosphere was thus improving, the actual economic condition was a bad as ever. The hardest times were experiences by the demobilized soldiers. They were the nation's scape-goat, and unemployment among them was serious. Industrial production was low, and employers turned down ex-service men for fear of public disapproval. The honest and serious-minded among the hard-pressed repatriates walked endlessly looking for a job, and when they did not find any they exchanged everything they had for food. Soon there were no more to be converted to food. Many ex-soldiers, however, found a way out in shady occupations and crimes. Lawlessness was rampant. Only the most enterprising kept themselves alive and still earned a livelihood legally.

My only chance for a decent job lay in the industrial field. Fortunately, after a year's waiting, a friend of mine introduced me to a manufacturing firm in a distant town near Nagoya. The company made automobiles. It appealed to me, and one early summer day I packed enough food to last several days and set out for an interview. In my pocket was a letter which read:

"We are interested in offering you a position. Before we come to a definite arrangement with you, however, will you consider the following matters? We have deep sympathy for the many hard experiences you have had during the war, but the position we have in mind requires that you be able to work without tension. Do you feel that you can do it? Another important item has to do with the fact that in the event that you are hired, it will become widely known. Both we and those who recommended you are of the opinion that every effort be made to avoid exploitation of your fame. Will you agree to this and co-operate with us? Please come for an interview at your earliest convenience."

The letter was signed by the manager of the Toyoda Automobile Manufacturing Company[24].

I came to Osaka Station in order to entrain to the town where the firm was. I stood one whole night in line waiting my turn to buy a ticket, then almost half a day in the long winding line to the platform. Finally I was on the platform. The train came in with an over-

---

[24] This was the old name for the company. Although founded by Kiichiro Toyoda in 1935, the name was changed to Toyota in 1937 since it took eight brush strokes (considered lucky) and because "toyoda" means "fertile rice paddies," hardly a modern image for a growing industrial company. [Ed.]

whelming noise and stopped. But even before it fully stopped, people began to push themselves into the coaches. The struggle was as ugly and as ruthless as any I had seen all my life. Women screamed, children cried, and the old ones fainted. Everyone stepped on everybody else. Many squeezed themselves through the glassless windows. Men helped push men through those windows when there was absolutely no room inside. People carried big bundles of food. As in my own case, these bundles meant something to eat for a long journey lasting several days. Ordinarily it would not take that long, but in those days of transportation jams, there was no telling when one could get on a train. Often the old and weak sat on the platform for a day and even three days.

While I was being pushed and squeezed I heard an American soldier yell, "Hey, you!"

He was not calling anyone in particular. It sounded more as if he was addressing the whole of Japan, for he had with him an old woman.

"Make room for this lady. She's been waiting for three days. Come on, come on. Move over. Let her in."

People moved their bodies back and forth, and she was able to get in – a miracle.

The real miracle was the American soldier. He was everywhere and everything. He could do things no Japanese could do. His word was law, and people admired him.

"I am getting old," the woman explained as she cried with happiness. "I just wanted to go to my son's home in the country and see my grandchildren before I died.

But I could not get on for three days. I was so hungry and tired that I thought I was going to die on the platform. Now I can see them. I am so grateful."

With passengers hanging on everywhere, the train pulled out. The toys in the woman's hands were all crushed and were of no use, but she made a gesture of a bow towards the American.

The G.I.'s had conquered Japan.

# 7. *Love and the Beginning of Freedom*

WHEN my return was spread over the papers, I received letter from many maidens. Most of the letters were written on very romantic paper by obviously young girls. They were first merely dreamy compositions, but gradually some of them grew into positive requests for correspondence and friendship. As the tone of the letters became more and more romantic, I became rather alarmed. Proposals were clearly indicated in some of them. Photographs and biographies were enclosed. At last one lady came to see me! She was tall and beautiful. But somehow I could not like her. I saw her for several minutes and asked her to excuse me. She went away disappointed.

The situation became serious. I felt that something had to be done, but I had no one in mind.

My father said, "I am thinking of your age. I must think about your marriage. I would like to hear what your wishes are. If you let me know what you would like us to do, I can rest in peace.

I felt that marriage was *my* problem. I thought that I

should decide this matter with my own free will. I could understand my parents' concern. They wanted me to have a normal life. I wanted to please my parents, too. I thought that marriage would be a fine finale to the turbulent career I had led. But I needed time to think through so many problems, new problems, life, society, the opposite sex.

My first step was clearly getting a job. To choose an occupation was a new experience. Until now I was letting fate run my life. To decide what to do by myself was a thrilling departure from my past habits. If I could break it by deliberately making a choice about a job, maybe I could choose my own wife, too.

"Please give me one year to pull myself together," I begged my parents.

Spring came to postwar Japan in 1946. The warm sun melted any hardness that was in human minds. The warmth of nature softened my heart and woke hibernating youth in me. The figures of attractive females began to make vivid impressions upon my mind. At night sentiments danced around in my dreams.

The war was gone from me. The barbed wire had disappeared from my visions. The old chain of the past was snapped loose and I was free. In my body was now flowing the vigorous blood of youth. I was free. I praised freedom. Free also were the butterflies that danced around among the flowers in the field. My eyes that watched them saw beautiful maidens instead.

Breathing the warm and free air of spring, I swung my hoe with all my might. Then in the dark soil under my feet, I saw worms of spring crawl sleepily. My brother and I laughed and enjoyed our happiness. His face was beaming with joy. He was also a repatriate, and for him a happy event was very near.

"May I get married before you do?" he had asked.

I had met his fiancée. She was pretty and modest. I blessed them both and wished them lots of happiness. But I felt a little restless afterward.

The warm breeze of spring touched my cheeks. Young men of the village went by whistling joyously. My mind was filled with thoughts of sweetness and romance. I bent down and pulled young green grass.

I paused at noon to sip my tea. I looked at the peaceful scene of spring before me. Everything was growing, the sun was warm, and the sky was light blue and full of larks.

I saw a straw hat moving in a neighbor's field. That straw hat belonged to a young lady. I had known that all along. I realized who the person was. She was Sadako. There was no question about it. I had heard a lot about her family.

Her father was a graduate of the Tokyo Imperial University. He was a judge. He was a good friend of my father. They were distant relatives as a matter of fact.

The judge lived in Hiroshima. Sadako grew up there. She had an elder brother and a sister. They were very happy. The family was well to do and the children knew no restrictions. When she was graduated from high school, she was hired as a secretary in a government office.

Then, on August 6, 1945, one bomb wiped out Hiroshima and her happiness. Her brother was killed. Her father died a few months later.

With two white boxes (containing symbolic remains of the deceased) her mother moved back to her ancestral home. That was how Sadako had come to live next to our farm. They were poor now. I thought that they were lonesome.

Sadako had never worked on a farm. She did not know the first thing about farming. And her awkward manners on the field had attracted curious attention of the villagers.

I was smoking a rationed cigarette. Then I was overcome by a desire to see the amateur farmer under the straw hat. So I rose and walked to her.

I saw her! It was only a glimpse. The complexion of her face was fair. Her nose was straight and of fine shape. The eyes with which she looked at me for a moment were large and round. There was a lovely smile in them.

I left. I thought, what a wonderful woman! She looked so beautiful and clever. Now I wanted to get that job more than ever.

When I returned from the trip, my father said to me:

"A friend of ours came to see me while you were gone, and you have a fine prospect of a very good match. The other party is Sadako. They say that they have studied your background and thoroughly approve of you. If you will say all right, the negotiations will be pushed quickly."

Sadako! Yes, she was the girl I had seen in the field.

My first impression was good. But why so quickly?

A job and marriage were the two important cornerstones of my future. They were now ready to be laid simultaneously.

"I would like to think it over, father. I would not consent right now although I certainly would not say no."

This man who had come with the marriage proposal was my former teacher. He was our family friend all right. He came to see me frequently and tried very hard to persuade me. He praised Sadako sky high. And he seemed very pleased with the role of go-between that he was playing.

Although I was in favor of the whole idea, I did not like to be rushed into it by other people. I deliberately thought of many negative angles. Sadako was a young girl, very innocent and perhaps rather ignorant of life's realities. Her mother was perhaps anxious to marry her off. Maybe Sadako was not so anxious to marry me herself. Just as in my case, she might be under another's pressure, I thought.

I stared at my reflection in the mirrorlike surface of the water in the field. I felt dizzy. I said to myself, "Don't yield to pressure. If you want to marry her, make up your mind by yourself and with her."

I asked for Sadako's papers. A health certificate, academic records, a brief biography, a certificate of her family background, all certified as to their accuracy, were delivered to me. I studied them carefully.

All this seemed rather formal. Yet, having spent my years of youth in a navy uniform, living on an island in the Inland Sea where there were no women, and having passed the most recent four years in a prison camp where there were no women, I had no previous experience with the opposite sex even in the most casual social sense, not to mention the physical, and thus lacked completely any qualifications to judge the lady under consideration. But I had to make a decision, if only to relieve my parents of anxiety and myself of the pressure.

Then one very hot day in summer I received a notice from the company. The job was now definite. I had to start working. I was going to become a useful and productive member of society. I thought that I should not let my past dictate to me any more. I was as much entitled to happiness as any other free man.

I took a big step. I wrote a letter to Sadako, asking her to associate with me as a friend. I received an affirmative reply. Thus ignoring busy talks of the villagers, Sadako and I went to a city for shopping. We were bashful and did not say very much the first time, but we were happy being together just the same.

A contract of marriage was exchanged between the two families. We were now formally engaged.

One day – it was a very hot day – Sadako and I went on a picnic in the mountains. Cicadas were chirping noisily all over the trees. When Sadako was not looking, I suddenly took her in my arms and gave her a strong kiss. She looked amazed, but with red hot cheeks she returned a nice, sweet, and equally strong kiss. While I held her firmly against my chest, her soft body seemed to vibrate with happiness.

# 8. *Skinny but Happy*

SADAKO and I were married on August 15, the first anniversary of peace. I was twenty-eight, and she was just right.

We moved to our present locality and we are living in a small apartment near the company. Making a living is extremely difficult, but we are optimistic. We have happiness and each other.

The world outside, however, is full of uncertainties. On the positive side we have a new Constitution which forbids war and guarantees the rights and dignity of the individual. Society is undergoing a bloodless revolution. The power of family monopolies in industry has been broken. The labor-management relationship is being democratized, replacing the old feudal system of bosses and ruthless exploitation. For these basic reforms the people are truly grateful to General MacArthur.

I often heard people say, "Life has brightened up since the end of the war. It's not easy to make a living, but we have hopes for the future. We have paid a heavy price for war, but considering the benefits of the Occupation, the defeat was really worthwhile."

Another said thoughtfully, "We must admit we do not know what democracy really is. But we have teachers who can show us. The important thing for us is not so much to understand democracy as a political theory as it is to question our conventional ideas and try to learn what is best for all concerned. As long as we have our directions set right, we shall learn. It will take many years, but we shall learn."

The International Tribunal in Tokyo was a constant topic of conversation. The most sensible interpretation was this statement heard in a private conversation:

"The trial of Tojo and others is not merely a trial of the top war criminals. It is a trial of us all, our ideas, and our traditional culture itself."

When we arrived here to work at the Toyoda company, I noticed those posters conspicuously displayed: "Down with the Reactionary Government! Join the Communist Party. Toyoda Cell Group."

I was to become a member of the personnel department. I realized that my task would not be very simple under those circumstances. But I could see from my vantage point how Communism operated in a local situation because I had to see almost everyone in the company's employ.

I believe that Communism in Japan has overplayed its hand. We know the Communists' tactics now. They infiltrate into small groups all over the country, particularly into industrial unions. But the only union to which our employees belonged voted to keep the party members out. Where a majority will is possible of realization, the Communists have little chance of control. Of course, secret meetings are constantly being held. A party representative visits them regularly from Tokyo and hands out the latest party line.

I am in charge of hiring new workers, and I ask them questions such as the following:

"Do you know anything about the Communist party?"

"Yes."

"Have you made a study of Communism?"

"No."

"Do you like the Communist party?"

"I do not like it, somehow."

"Do you agree with the principles of Communism?"

"There are some good things about Communism, but I don't like the way they advocate and use violence."

"In what way do they use violence?"

"I don't know."

"You don't know?"

"Not very well. But they seem to want to overthrow the emperor by force. The emperor, I think, is essential to the people of Japan."

From this somewhat incoherent conversation, it seems obvious that most people do not have any deep understanding of Communism. They just vaguely dislike it. I think this is a dangerous state of mind. The masses could be swayed one way or the other easily.

The recent "victory" of the Communist party in the

general election was not so much a deliberate change of mind on the part of the people as a fear created by the international situation. What had happened in China influenced many inarticulate people to assume that Communism was spreading all over Asia, and if that was the case they wanted to be on the winning side.

As long as Communism plays the role of the champion of democracy, there will be confusion in this country. The serious-minded people wish to know the real difference. In the meantime a fear of World War III grips the minds of the people.

The only certain thing in Japan is that the old Japan is dying.

One day when I was ready to go home, I was told that someone wanted to see me.

When I went to the reception room, I found an old friend. After the greeting was exchanged, he asked:

"What do you think of the news?"

"What news?" I said innocently.

"You don't know? It's that thing, you know?"

"What thing?"

"This," said my visitor, and he wrung his neck as in hanging. He was referring to the hanging of the top war criminals.

"Oh, so they have done it now, have they?"

I sat still and stared at a corner of the table. So the end of the seven Class A criminals had come[25]. I felt as if I were being pressed against a wall.

"So they have been killed," I repeated to myself.

---

[25] On December 23, 1948, former Japanese Premier Hideki Tojo and six other top Japanese leaders were hung for war crimes. [Ed.]

There was no denying it any more. The leaders of the old Japan were dead. I was a part of that Japan. Then suddenly the face of Tojo flashed in my mind, and I came to myself.

"I knew this was going to take place, but somehow I have forgotten it."

"You don't sound like yourself. The radio has been telling us all day."

"I've been so busy all day. No one at the company mentioned it."

"Just as well. What was due has come to pass, that's all."

I nodded. What was due has come to pass, that was all. Somehow a heavy burden of lead seemed to get off my chest.

The past was dying.

One day I received a letter from another friend. It read:

"I was walking in a street in Kyoto not long ago. I saw a familiar figure. He was bald-headed and was mumbling something unintelligible. People paid no more than passing attention to him. But I recognized him as Commander Nakamune."

The past was dying.

The birth of a new Japan, however, is not without pains. The battle of ideas is going on relentlessly. Old ideas are fighting new ideas. It is a losing battle, but they will not give up easily. But one by one the old ideas must die. When the figure of Tojo in uniform disappeared for good, the symbol of militarism had fallen. Feudalism must go, too. The idea that a man can use another person as a means for his end must be replaced by something else. I have an idea. It is not a well-formulated idea as yet, but it is something that I had learned while living in America.

I can trace it step by step because my idea did not become mine through reading or hearing about it. It came by four years of experience. My steps were these: all-out attack, failure, capture, a sense of dilemma, mental struggle, attempts at suicide, failure again, self-contempt, deep disillusionment, despair and melancholy, reflections, desire to learn and yearning for truth, meditation, rediscovering myself, self-encouragement, discovery of a new duty, freedom through love, a desire for reconstruction.

I claim no credit for this transformation. I wish to preach to no one. I only hope that this will show to all others who were once prisoners and to all who have received us with varying moods that man is capable of being made anew.

This is not a plea in behalf of former prisoners of war. I am aware of a few instances where former prisoners of war have gone astray. I only ask that the people of Japan do not generalize about all ex-prisoners by the actions of a few among them. I can understand also why some of us do commit crimes. We deplore them even more than the rest of the country does. Yet we, who have done all we could except that we failed to commit suicide, beg our people to forgive us. I have not written this to have our names restored upon the roll of honor, least of all, mine.

The idea that I learned, which I wish to share with

123

all my fellow countrymen, is that man can and should live in pursuit of happiness.

I met an American soldier who said, "I hope the war will be over soon, so I can buy a car, a refrigerator, and electric freezer, and automatic washing machine, and get married." Although we would probably not think ever of buying those mechanical goods, we might try to find happiness in life. The American attitude towards machines and gadgets was an intriguing one. It could be overdone, and yet one might consider those conveniences as means of creating a more abundant life.

Americans love freedom greatly. Freedom is their history. This idea must have come from Christianity. I understand that they jealously guard their religious freedom. In fact it was for this that the first settlers came to America. There is a Statue of Liberty in the New York Harbor. The statue is the symbol of the American spirit. What is the symbol of the new Japan?

Democracy in American is scientific. Americans use a questionnaire for almost everything. They want to find out how many people like this and how many people like that. What the questionnaire finds out becomes the will of the majority. Although this fact-finding method is not the only one used to determine what people want, it is a very American technique of doing things. Voting in an election is the same idea.

I noticed also that in America the woman is respected. One day a group of newspaper reporters came to our camp. When they were leaving the room, the commanding officer said, "Ladies, please." The women reporters went out first, followed by the commanding officer, myself, and the men reporters. When the President of the United States issued a message to the armed forces, his first words were, "To the women and men in our armed forces." I thought this was very interesting. I do not agree with some people in Japan who say that in a democracy the woman is superior to the man. The truth is that she is an equal of the male.

I read Mr. Willkie's *One World*. I know that there are many books like it in America. World-mindedness is an important element of American democracy. We have much to learn in this respect, too.

In conversations with Americans I often heard the expression, "You are right." We Japanese do not say this very much. When we talk with superiors we agree verbally and we expect our inferiors to agree with us. In America ranks are not important. No matter who says it, if what he says is right, the other person admits it is right. This shows how open-minded Americans are. This is something we lack.

As an interesting companion phrase to "you are right," there is another often used expression, "maybe." It is a questioning mind. It is good to have such an attitude. If we had a more questioning mind, we might have averted many of our past mistakes.

I observed other characteristics: the adventurous, "let's try it" mind; idealism and realism; the business-like mind and the fun-loving mind; independence and co-operativeness; the carefree mind and conscientiousness. All these blend to make up the American mind.

There are excesses and abuses. Yet through it all runs the American individual in pursuit of happiness. He is not for himself along, however. He is aware of the right of the other fellow. That is why everybody can be and is happy.

A mere imitation leads us astray. Jazz and dancing are sweeping Japan. But people who dance are not necessarily learning democracy. Democracy seems to be a more serious business. I do not understand it too well, but I think it must have something to do with the rights of men. That is my idea. I learned it as a prisoner. It was the best education of my life.

Japan is tending to be a democracy, but all ideas in the new Japan are not democratic. Among the new ideas that are fighting the old is Communism. Because Communists always use the word "democracy," we often get confused. I know Communism only through what I see the Communists do. I will keep a questioning mind. "Maybe, but…"

I have said enough.

* * *

In September, 1947 our first child was born. We named her Yoshiko. She is growing rapidly. I cannot say that she is very healthy. As I write these concluding lines, she is sound asleep. I look at her and feel sorry that she is so skinny because I cannot provide for her adequately.

My wife Sadako is sitting between me and the baby. She is mending my trousers. She is also skinny and pale, but she is as beautiful as ever. So we are all skinny, like most of the hard-working people in Japan, but we are optimistic. Above all, we are very happy.

# # #

# Appendix

## The Submarine Attack on Pearl Harbor

In addition to waves of torpedo planes, dive bombers, high-altitude bombers, fighter aircraft, the Imperial Japanese Navy plan included sending five battery-powered midget submarines into Pearl Harbor to attack underwater as well as stationing twenty-six large submarines outside the harbor to torpedo any ships that might try to head out into open water.

The United States Navy considered Pearl Harbor to be naturally protected from submarines due to its shallow depth of 40'. The harbor was protected with an anti-submarine net, but this was mainly to prevent enemy submarines from getting close enough to fire a torpedo into the main harbor.

The attack plan called for the midget submarines to enter the harbor under cover of darkness, presumably by following closely behind American ships while the nets were temporarily open. The subs were to take up pre-established positions and wait on the bottom until the main air attack before firing their two torpedoes at their predetermined targets.

After the attack the midget subs were supposed to navigate their way out of the harbor and re-unite with their mother subs near the island of Lanai.

They were also provided with maps of Oahu in case they had to scuttle their submarines and escape on land.

Map of Pearl Harbor found in Sakamaki's submarine

It was not supposed to be a suicide mission. Admiral Yamamoto was said to have told the sailors, "You will not complete your mission by dying, so please come back alive after releasing the torpedoes and work another day."

However, everyone involved knew the midget submarine attack would be incredibly dangerous and very likely fatal.

None of the five midget subs made it to the rendezvous spot. Ensign Sakamaki is the only known survivor of the midget submarine attack on Pearl Harbor.

## The Five Midget Subs

The midget submarines utilized in the attack on Pearl Harbor by the Imperial Japanese Navy were built in the Kure Naval Dockyard in Japan in 1938-1941, and were known as a Type "A" Kō-Hyōteki (little target) submarines.

Various means of identifying the midgets have been used over the years. The Navy numbered them "A-E" based on the order they were identified. They're also referred to as the small boats (tou) of the associated I-class mother ship.

The submarine crews (from left to right)

| Midget Sub | Skipper (seated) | Crewman |
|---|---|---|
| *I-16tou* | Masaharu Yokoyama | Sadamu Kamita |
| *I-18tou* | Shigemi Furuno | Shigenori Yokoyama |
| *I-20tou* | Akira Hiroo | Yoshio Katayama |
| *I-22tou* | Naoji Iwasa | Naokichi Sasaki |
| *I-24tou* | Kazuo Sakamaki | Kiyoshi Inagaki |

### I-20tou / M-20 / Midget A / "The Ward Midget"

This midget sub was launched from mother sub I-20 at 3am about 5 miles from the harbor entrance, and the crew consisted of Ensign Akira Hiroo and Yoshio Katayama.

At 5:45 am the navy cargo carrier USS *ANTARES* (AG-10) spotted a suspicious object behind their ship which was also noticed by a Catalina PBY seaplane flying overhead. By 6:45 am the destroyer USS *WARD* (DD-139) had arrived on the scene and fired at the partially submerged submarine, piercing the conning tower with a 4-inch shell.

This was the first shot fired in the Pearl Harbor attack and the first shot fired by the United States in World War II.

The shell did not explode, but as the sub started to sink the ship also dropped depth charges.

In 2002 a University of Hawaii submersible research vehicle located the sunken sub in 1,330 feet of water about five miles off Pearl Harbor after years of searching for it. Both torpedoes were still onboard, and there was a hole in the conning tower which confirmed it was the midget submarine hit and sunk by the USS *WARD*.

It is believed to be Hiroo and Katayama's midget sub. Their remains are still inside the submarine which lies undisturbed on the ocean floor.

### I-22tou / M-22 / Midget B / "The Monaghan Midget"

This was the second submarine sighted by the Navy during the main attack, and this one was inside Pearl Harbor in the North Channel off the northwest side of Ford Island.

The midget sub was launched shortly after 1am from the I-22, with Lt Naoji Iwasa as skipper and crewman Naokichi, Sasaki, about nine miles from the harbor entrance.

About 30 minutes into the air attack the sub's periscope was spotted by sailors aboard the USS *ZANE* (DMS-14). Several of the nearby ships opened fire on it and the USS *MONAGHAN* (DD-354), underway at the time, gave chase with the intention to ram it.

The submarine fired a torpedo at the USS *CURTISS* (AV-4) which caused the sub to momentarily broach. The conning tower was hit by a 5-inch shell and raked by .50 caliber machine-gun fire. The torpedo missed and hit a dock on the Pearl City peninsula. The sub fired its last torpedo at the destroyer, but it barely missed to starboard and exploded on the shore of Ford Island.

The USS *MONAGHAN* rammed the submarine and dropped two depth charges that blew the midget submarine to the surface before quickly sinking.

It is believed to be Lt. Iwasa's submarine since a shirt sleeve with the Japanese naval rank insignia of a full Lieutenant was found floating in the harbor and he was the only submarine skipper with that rank.

The sub was raised about three weeks after the attack but it was in pretty bad shape. After salvaging a few parts the submarine was used as fill for the reconstruction of a submarine dock at Ford Island. There are conflicting reports whether the crew was buried with the sub or not.

It was accidently uncovered in 1952 but was left in place due to extensive corrosion caused by chlorine gas from the old batteries.

### I-24tou / M-24 / Midget C / HA-19 / "Sakamaki's Midget"

After Kazuo Sakamaki and Kiyoshi Inagaki abandoned their submarine it was dislodged from the reef and hauled up onto the beach near Bellows Air Field on December 8, 1941. Inagaki's body washed up onshore the next day.

The scuttling charge was removed and the submarine was taken to Pearl Harbor and carefully dismantled and then extensively studied and documented by the U.S. Navy.

On December 26, 1941, the US Navy's Submarine Squadron Four issued a detailed 76-page report of their investigation. In addition to annotated photographs of the interior and exterior, it also included copies of Sakamaki's log and other data from the captured sub.

*US Navy*

COMPOSITE PICTURE

*US Navy*

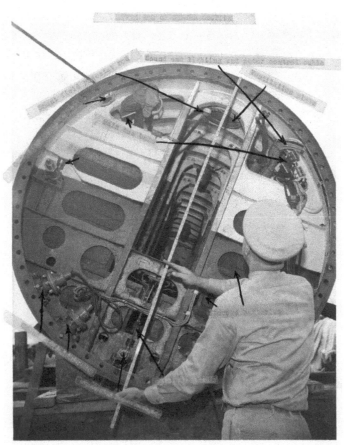

*US Navy*

*US Navy*

*US Navy*

*US Navy*

*US Navy*

*US Navy*

*US Navy*

*US Navy*

Once the military finished their investigations, damaged parts of the submarine were restored with parts from the midget sub destroyed by the USS Monaghan in Pearl Harbor (I-22tou) and it was shipped to the Mare Island Naval Shipyard near San Francisco.

The interior was cleaned out and electric lights were installed along with fake engines and batteries. Two mannequin crew members with fierce Samurai expressions were also added, and twenty-two small viewing windows were cut into the hull on each side.

The sub was mounted on a trailer and on October 27, 1942 began a tour of 2,000 cities in 41 states as the catalyst for a hugely successful War Bond fundraising effort. (See http://mirc.sc.edu/islandora/object/usc%3A26031). With two drivers alternating every six hours, the sub was taken to eight to fifteen towns a day across the US.

# SEE SUB— — SINK SAME!

# JAP SUICIDE-SUB

## Comes to Ann Arbor Saturday, July 17

**This captured Jap Sub will be on display in Ann Arbor in the 100 block of North Fourth Ave., opposite the courthouse, from 4 p.m. to 10 p.m. Saturday, July 17.**

See 76,500 pounds---81 feet---of fanatical fiendishness. See one of the ships in which two of our enemies volunteer to accept death in order to blow up their objectives. See this Japanese Suicide Submarine and realize what a vicious, tricky, desperate enemy our boys are fighting in the Pacific! It is sent on tour of Michigan by the U. S. Treasury Department as a mark of appreciation for the fine job you did in the Second War Loan. Every extra War Bond it causes you to purchase during the next ten days will bear a special commemorative stamp, reading, "Saw Sub---Sank Same"---for that's what your bonds are doing every day! Let's hit them harder---let's depth-bomb them to the bottom of the sea---let's show them what an aroused, all-out America can do!

## Buy An EXTRA WAR BOND and Depth-Bomb The Axis!

This advertisement sponsored by the following firms:

*Ann Arbor News*

*Ralph Gerbens / Connie Gerbens Stark*

*Ralph Gerbens / Connie Gerbens Stark*

*US Library of Congress*

Adults could peek inside the submarine if they purchased a minimum of $1 worth of War Savings Stamps. Children could see inside for a 25-cent War Savings Stamp.

It has been said that the war bond tour with Sakamaki's Japanese submarine raised enough money to pay for the repair of all the ships damaged in the Pearl Harbor attack.

After the war the submarine sat for a while at the Naval Pier in Chicago. It was later on display at the US Naval Station in Key West, Florida, and then moved to the Key West Lighthouse and Military Museum.

In 1989 HA-19 was declared a United States National Historic Landmark.

In 1990 Sakamaki's submarine was moved to the National Museum of the Pacific War in Fredericksburg, Texas, where it was restored and remains on display to this day.

*National Museum of the Pacific War*

For a virtual tour go to: https://youtu.be/xVAorYNncvw).

One of its original propellers is on exhibit at the Pacific Fleet Submarine Museum at Pearl Harbor.

*Gary Coover*

Sakamaki's "kai-gunto" sword was found in the submarine and given to the US Naval Academy Museum in Annapolis, MD, by Rear Admiral Thomas Withers, Commander, Submarines, US Pacific Fleet.

*Gary Coover*

The sword is displayed next to the top portion of the Monaghan Midget's (I-22tou) periscope.

The complete periscope from Sakamaki's submarine is now in The Mariners' Museum and Park in Newport News, Virginia. A similar periscope is also on display in the "Attack" Exhibit Gallery at the Pearl Harbor Visitor Center in Honolulu.

*Richard Kitterman*

### I-18tou / M-18 / Midget D / "The Keehi Lagoon Midget"

Very little is known about the activities of this submarine after it was launched about 2am from mother submarine I-18 about 13 miles outside Pearl Harbor. The skipper was Shigemi Furuno with crewman Shigenori Yokoyama.

The submarine was discovered accidentally in 75 feet of water off Keehi Lagoon in 1960 during routine training by Navy divers.

Video footage of the sub being recovered can be seen at https://youtu.be/AeCEceqYNcA, courtesy of the United States National Archives.

Both torpedoes were still on board and the hatch had been opened from the inside.

There appeared to be evidence of depth charge damage inside, but the only trace left of the crew was a pair of coveralls, one boot, one glove, a rubber-soled sandal, several wrenches and an empty bottle of sake.

The fate of the crew is unknown.

Since the forward section still contained both torpedoes, it was cut off and disposed of at sea.

At the request of the Japanese Government the remainder of the midget submarine was returned to Japan where it was restored and placed on permanent display at the Imperial Japanese Naval Academy at Eta Jima near Hiroshima.

### I-16tou / M-16 / Midget E / "The Fifth Midget"

This midget sub was the first one launched by the Special Attack Unit right after midnight on the night of December 7, 1941. The skipper was Masaharu Yokoyama and crewman was Sadamu Kamita.

At approximately 10:30pm on the night of December 7, almost 24 hours later, the I-16 mother sub received a radio message from the midget sub indicating "successful attack". Shortly after midnight another message was received saying "unable to navigate".

What happened between the launch of this sub and the finding of it in three pieces about three miles outside Pearl Harbor between 1992 and 2001 has been the subject of much conjecture and controversy.

Discovered by the Hawai'i Undersea Research Laboratory (HURL) on an early search for the "Ward Midget", this sub had obviously been salvaged elsewhere and cut into three pieces and dumped outside Pearl Harbor. Holes had been punched in the hull and steel cables were still attached to the pieces.

Both torpedoes had been fired. The hatch had been opened from the inside. There was no sign of the crew.

It was dumped in an area full of hundreds of pieces of discarded military war materials.

To date, no records of any previous salvage operation of this submarine have been located, but it is suspected that its original location might have been where a massive and deadly explosion occurred in Pearl Harbor's West Loch amphibious staging area in 1944.

Since the midget sub was found amidst the wreckage of the explosion cleanup, some have theorized that the sub was coincidentally found in the cleanup area, picked up, cut into more manageable sections and then dumped in the ocean with the other debris under strict wartime secrecy.

If this scenario is the case, then this midget sub also made it into Pearl Harbor and perhaps managed to fire on Battleship Row.

A wartime photograph taken by a Japanese airman during the attack possibly shows a midget submarine in the act of firing its torpedoes. Some believe the USS *WEST VIRGINIA* might have been hit by the first torpedo.

Did the other torpedo hit the USS *OKLAHOMA,* or maybe the USS *ARIZONA* as some suggest, or was it a dud as reportedly found later by the Navy that matched the larger Type 97 torpedo fired by the midget submarines?

Either way, this submarine crew might have fired at least one successful torpedo and then scuttled their ship afterwards in the relatively quiet West Loch. This could also explain the later radio message indicating a successful attack.

The submarine has not been re-salvaged and remains in three pieces in 1,575 feet of water off Pearl Harbor.

# The Nine Hero Gods

Shortly after the Pearl Harbor attack the Japanese propaganda machine declared the nine midget submarine crewmen who died in the Pearl Harbor attack to be "hero gods" and posthumously promoted them two ranks

A formal navy funeral service was held on April 8, 1942, and this special memorial photo montage was created to honor their sacrifice.

It was even claimed that one of these heroic midget submarines had sunk the USS *ARIZONA*.

There was conspicuously no mention of Kazuo Sakamaki.

He had disgraced the nation with his capture and the seizure of his top-secret submarine.

## Sakamaki's Post WWII Career

Sakamaki wrote an account of his wartime experiences that was published by Shinchosa Publishing Company as "Horyo Daiichi-go" (Prisoner of War Number One) in 1949.

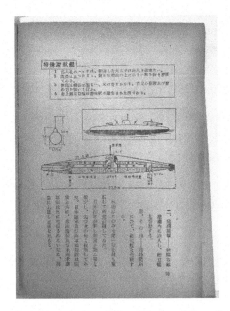

*Courtesy Japanese Cultural Center of Hawaii*

After completing his memoir he became a fairly private person and only occasionally spoke or wrote about his time in the war.

Sakamaki went on to become Production Chief of Toyota's Export Division in Nagoya, and between 1969 and 1983 he was the president of Toyota's Brazilian subsidiary.

He retired in 1987 after 40 years with Toyota.

*Associated Press*

In May 1991, Sakamaki was invited to attend a historical conference at the National Museum of the Pacific War in Fredericksburg, Texas, where he reportedly wept when he saw his old midget submarine for the first time in 50 years.

*National Museum of the Pacific War*

After a long, successful life, Kazuo Sakamaki passed away on November 29, 1999 in Toyota, Aichi Prefecture, Japan. He was 81 years old.

# Recommended Reading

Burlingame, Burl. *Advance Force Pearl Harbor.* US Naval Institute Press, 2002.

Craddock, John. *First Shot: The Untold Story of the Japanese Minisubs that Attacked Pearl Harbor.* Camden, McGraw-Hill, 2006.

Delgado, Kerby, Van Tilburg, Price, Varmer, Cremer, Matthews. *The Lost Submarines of Pearl Harbor.* College Station, Texas A&M University Press, 2017.

www.i16tou.com

www.combinedfleet.com/Pearl.htm

www.navsource.org

http://mirc.sc.edu/islandora/object/usc%3A26031 (Sakamaki's submarine on war bond tour)

# Acknowledgements

Many thanks to these individuals and organizations for their historic preservation efforts and/or permission to include photographs:

Associated Press, Connie Gerbens Stark, Historic Naval Ships Association, Japanese Cultural Center of Hawaii, National Border Patrol Museum, National Museum of the Pacific War, Thomas Hale Hamilton Library of the University of Hawai'i, US Air Force, US Library of Congress, US National Archives, US Naval History and Heritage Command, US Naval Historical Foundation, USS Bowfin Submarine Museum and Park, World War II Valor in the Pacific National Monument at Pearl Harbor Hawaii.

## Toru Matsumoto, Translator

Born in Japan in 1913, Matsumoto studied at Meiji Gakuin in Tokyo, Union Theological Seminary in New York, became an ordained minister, and obtained a Ph.D. in Education from Columbia University.

He served on the staffs of the Committee on Friendly Relations Among Foreign Students and the Committee on Resettlement of Japanese-Americans, and he was a former general secretary and editor of the Japanese Student Christian Association of North America. He is the author of *The Seven Stars, A Brother Is a Stranger*, and *Beyond Prejudice: A Story of the Church and Japanese Americans.*

## Gary R. Coover, Editor

Researcher and historian Gary Coover has long been fascinated with the Pearl Harbor midget submarine story, even more so after moving to Honolulu several years ago.

While researching a completely different project he discovered a copy of Sakamaki's book in the Hawaiian Collection at the Thomas Hale Hamilton Library at the University of Hawai'i.

Realizing the importance of keeping this memoir available to military historians and the general public, he recreated the look and feel of the original plus added notes and photographs to illustrate and update the events in Sakamaki's important wartime memoir.